3D PRINTING STEP BY STEP

3D DESIGN TUTORIALS AND COMMON MISTAKES IN 3D PRINTING WITH SOLUTIONS.

CARMELITO ANDRADE

Contents

Acknowledgements

Writing a book is harder than I thought and more rewarding than I could have ever imagined. I would like to express my gratitude to many people, who provided support, talked things over, read and offered valuable comments.

I owe a special thanks to my Technical Editor, Savira Travasso, who assisted with editing and feedback. And Maclean Barretto for proofreading.

I'm eternally grateful to the 3D printing community on the world wide web, for all their support and helpful blog posts, especially in the first couple of years of my 3D printing journey in 2012-13. And many thanks to all the active community members, who unselfishly post their research, blogs about their issues, reply to the forum posts and encourage beginners to get into the 3D printing space.

In addition, for the cover of the book, I would thank my friend Krishanu Banerjee, for agreeing to patiently sit through a 3D scan of himself, which was then converted to a 3D design file to create a mold. The mold was then 3D printed so that wax can be poured into it, to create a candle.

Who Is This Book For?

I applaud and thank you for buying this book and would like to believe that you have already taken steps to buy a 3D printer or have a 3D design in mind and have located a friend/relative who has a 3D printer. Or you have spoken to your teacher at school/college after seeing the 3D printer at the corner of your computer lab/ library.

This book introduces you to 3D printing and will guide you through the complete process of designing and printing an object. Suitable for young students in 8th grade and higher. The last few chapters will give insight into common mistakes that beginners tend to make. And help explain the future/potential of this technology.

In addition, this is an ideal book for a Hobbyist/Maker who wants to learn about all the 3D printing terminology/jargon. And also want to hit the ground running, by quickly designing 3D objects for their project. A free simple web-based program called Tinkercad is ideal for this. You will only need an internet browser like Chrome and don't have to go through the hassle of installing and paying for expensive 3D software.

The book will also come in handy at any level of expertise, especially the last few chapters. It deals with common printing problems, how to tackle them, and general printer maintenance to ensure your printer lasts and keeps running for a long time.

Note For Parents On 3d Printing

3D printers allow students to design and create 3D objects, from simple things like custom keychains and phone cases to complex mechanical objects. They're a fantastic tool for STEM(Science, Technology, Engineering, and Maths) because they provide hands-on lessons integrating technology, engineering, maths, art, and other subjects. Moreover, 3D-printing projects encourage creativity, collaboration, and problem-solving.

To print a 3D object, students use one of the three ways to create a digital file.

- If a 3D scanner is available, they scan and replicate something that exists.
- They download a template of a pre-designed object from the internet from 3D printing community websites.
- They use a Computer-Aided Design (CAD) modeling program to design an original object. In this book, we use a simple web-based program called Tinkercad. There is no need to install software on your computer, you just need the latest chrome browser.

Once students produce a digital file, they send it to the 3D printer, just as they would a document/pdf file. Most 3D printers have a window, allowing students to watch as the printer creates the object, layer by layer, using a plastic filament.

Students will also learn a lot of new words when they begin to study STEM and topics like 3D printing. A great deal of technical vocabulary is used in the book, names of equipment and various 3D printing terminology is explained.

CHAPTER I

What is 3D printing?

Since the 1400s, when Michel Angelo was creating astonishing sculptures from marble, our way of making things has involved taking a larger block of material and chipping it down to create a smaller, final piece. In the modern-day, this mostly continues, with CNC machines and laser cutters, creating final pieces by removing parts from a larger block of material. These methods are known as subtractive manufacturing, as they subtract bits to get to the final part, which sometimes leads to a lot of waste material.

3D printing is different. Instead, 3D printing builds parts from scratch by either depositing melted materials or solidifying or melting resins or powders to form the part. Rather than chipping extra material, 3D printers deposit only the exact amount of material required leaving minimal waste and saving money on excess material. For this reason, 3D printing is also known as additive manufacturing. It adds to create a part rather than removing bits from a larger block, this is significantly better for the environment and mother earth.

3D printed parts are created three-dimensionally by printing tiny horizontal layers of material, layer-by-layer, on top of each other to build a larger part gradually. Each layer may be as small as 0.01 mm in depth, which means hundreds of layers may be required to create a part that is 5 cm tall.

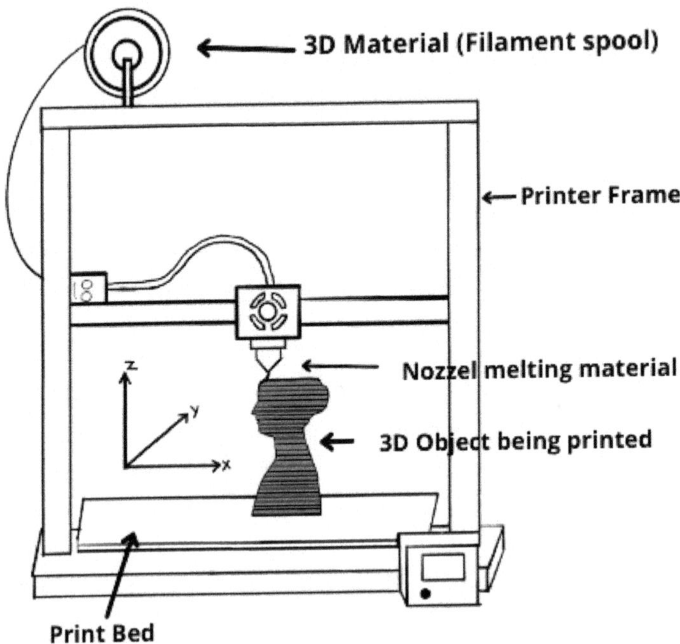

The word "printing" might make you think of a computer paper printer at home, which is used to print pdfs, word documents, etc. 3D printing is a little different. Your paper printer has only X and Y axis, while a 3D printer in addition to X and Y axis also has a Z-axis for depth.

> "*From Wikipedia, here is the definition, "3D printing, or additive manufacturing, is the construction of a three-dimensional object from a CAD(Computer-Aided Designed) model or a digital 3D model. The term "3D printing" can refer to a variety of processes in which material is deposited, joined or solidified under computer control to create a three-dimensional object, with the material being added together (such as plastics, liquids or powder grains being fused), typically layer by layer."*"

Based on the above definition of 3D printing from Wikipedia, you already will have quite a few questions in your mind.

- What is Additive Manufacturing?
- What is CAD(Computer-Aided Design)?
- Where can you get a 3D model?
- What if you decide to make your own 3D model?
- How do you print 3D models?
- What are the materials used by the 3D printer?
- What are the common 3D printing technologies?
- Is it possible to scan and print a real object?
- Where are the 3D printers being used today?
- Do you really need to buy a 3D printer?

So let's get started by answering the questions which will allow you to get familiar with the common terminology used in the 3D printing space.

What is Additive Manufacturing?

Additive manufacturing is the process of creating an object by building it one layer at a time. It is the opposite of subtractive manufacturing, in which an object is produced by cutting away at a solid block of material until the final product is complete. Technically, additive manufacturing can refer to a process where a product is created by building something up, such as moulding, but it typically refers to 3-D printing.

To create an object using additive manufacturing, you must first create a design. This is typically done using CAD. The software then translates the design into a layer by layer framework for the additive manufacturing machine to follow. This is sent to the 3D printer, which immediately creates the object.

Note: The two other manufacturing techniques are Formative and Subtractive manufacturing.

Formative manufacturing is best suited for high volume production of the same part. Raw material like plastic or metal is melted down and extruded into a mould/casting or pressed or pulled into the desired shape. As you guessed, the price of the product sold in the market will be low, but the setup cost and machine are going to be high.

Subtractive Manufacturing is best suited for parts with relatively simple geometry. This type of manufacturing begins with a block of solid material, for example, metal, wood, etc. You then use cutting tools to remove material to achieve the final shape. Examples of such machines are CNC mills, Lathe, Laser cutters etc.

What is CAD(Computer-Aided Design)?

CAD refers to computers being used to assist the design process in industries. With CAD software, it's possible to build an entire model in an imaginary space, letting you visualise properties like height, width, distance, material, or colour before the model is used for a particular application. In the case of 3D printing, the CAD software exports an STL(Standard Triangle Language or sometimes also referred to as Standard Tessellation Language) file.

One of the earliest primary tools in CAD has evolved over the past few decades. It is called AutoCAD. AutoCAD has become extremely popular in drafting, engineering, and design, from jointers and rafters in carpentry to cutting plastics or other materials for custom parts. Large and small businesses have been integrating AutoCAD and its capabilities into their business processes since its release in 1982. However, one of the reasons that people look for alternatives to AutoCAD is its high cost structure. Various tools like Tinkercad are free and provide some functionality for money-minded users. As part of our 3D design tutorials in the book in chapter 6, we will use Autodesk Tinkercad to design and export STL files because it is a web-based tool and is free to use.

The other popular CAD tools you can design in are - FreeCAD, Fusion 360, Solidworks, OpenSCAD, Rhino, SketchUp etc.

Where can you get a 3D model?

If you intend to 3D print a model, that doesn't mean you always have to start designing from scratch. Tons of websites offer (both free and premium) 3D models to download. Here are some websites to get 3D models which you can use with your 3D printer

- Thingiverse.com
- Yeggi.com

- MyMinifactory.com
- Shapeways.com
- Pineshape.com

Thingiverse is probably one of the biggest and most popular databases. It has a very active maker community and offers free-to-use STL files only. You don't even need to open an account to download a 3D model from their site. Sometimes the database can seem slightly less organised than the cleaner and more straightforward design of websites like Pinshape. Based on the last count, Thingiverse has over 610,780 3D models for users to choose from.

Yeggi is a search engine for 3D printable models. Yeggi scans all the website databases mentioned above and many more for 3D printable files. So if you want to search the 'Google' of 3D models, this is the right website.

Shapeways allows users without 3D printers, to design and upload 3D printable files, and Shapeways prints the objects for them. Users can have objects printed in over 55 materials and finishes, these include plastics, precious metals, steel, food-safe materials, etc. The website also offers Designers to sell their own designs to be 3D printed on demand for customers. Shapeways handles the financial transaction, manufacture, distribution and customer service. And profits go to the 3D designer.

What if you decide to make your own model?

All you need to make your own model is CAD software. We are going to understand the basics of CAD software called Tinkercad which is available as a web-based application in Chapter VII. The plan is to design a keychain with your own name and a few other 3D models. Tinkercad is an ideal CAD tool to learn to grasp the concepts of 3D design. Once you are comfortable you can try out more complex tools like Fusion 360, SketchUp, and Solidworks which have a licensing cost associated with it.

Tinkercad is a browser-based 3D design application geared towards beginners. The software features an intuitive block-building concept, allowing you to develop models from a set of basic shapes. Tinkercad is full of tutorials and guides to aid any aspiring novices to get to the designs they're looking for. It even allows you to share and export files with ease. With a library of literally millions of files, users can find shapes that suit them best and manipulate them as they wish. Even though it can be a bit too simple to the point of limitation, it serves as a great way to learn about 3D modeling. And the best part is that it is free to use.

Fusion 360 by Autodesk is a cloud-based 3D CAD program that utilises the power of the cloud to bring design teams together and collaborate on complex projects. Another advantage of the cloud platform is that Fusion 360 stores the entire history of the model, including its changes. Numerous design options are available, including free-form, solid, and mesh modeling. Fusion 360 operates on a monthly payment subscription basis. The developers also regularly update the features making them better, as new instalments come along. It runs on multiple platforms like Windows and Mac and allows users to access their information wherever they want.

Blender covers many facets of 3D creation, including modeling, animation, and simulation. This open-source software is ideal for users who feel ready to transition from animation to designing complex 3D models. Blender is a free 3D modeling software initially created for 3D animation and rendering using polygonal modeling techniques. Despite its origins as software for artists, it is considered quite accessible. Though this is a feature-rich program which includes tools for sculpting, animation, simulation, rendering, motion tracking, and video editing, the learning curve can be steep.

SketchUp is another good modeling software because it maintains that balance between usability and functionality, making it ideal for most skill levels. The software has an easy learning curve, and there are advanced features available for professionals at an extra cost. It is perfect for designing interior and exterior architectural projects and has tools for various other purposes. Anything complex can take quite a while, but simpler designs aren't too time-consuming. A freeware version, SketchUp Make, and a paid version with additional functionality, SketchUp Pro, are also available.

SolidWorks is a CAD program often used by professional 3D designers. There are a plethora of advanced features included, such as design validation tools and reverse engineering. Like Fusion 360, Solidworks tends towards the industrial side of things, and both these software are fierce competitors. It is practical and detailed. For the pricing, you have yearly subscriptions and a way to purchase perpetual licence.

How do you print 3D models?

In addition to your CAD tool used to design 3D models and export them into a compatible format, primarily an STL file, you will also need another software/tool that executes a 3D printer.

Slicer software is the easiest way to go from a 3D model to a printed part because they take a CAD model, slices it into layers, and turns the model into G-code, which acts as an instruction set for the 3D printer. The slicer software also includes 3D printer settings like temperature, layer height, print speed, etc., to the G-code. The 3D printer can read this G-code and make the model layer by layer following the instructions set in the G-code to setup. There are a bunch of slicing software that you can use, like – Cura, Slic3r, Simplify3D, Repetier, etc.

Cura is developed by Ultimaker and can be used with almost any 3D printer because it is an open-source slicer. The program is ideal for beginners because it is intuitive and fast. Most of all, it's easy to use. More advanced users can access a further 200 settings to refine their prints.

Slic3r is another open-source slicer software, which includes real-time incremental slicing, 3D preview, and more. It is one of the most widely used 3D printing software tools. The incremental real-time slicing ensures that when you change a setting, the slicing doesn't need to start from scratch. Only the G-code for affected parts is recalculated. The end result is a fast, flexible and precise slicing program.

Simplify3D is an extremely powerful premium slicing tool that helps you drastically improve the quality of 3D prints. Not only does Simplify3D slice your CAD into layers, it also corrects any problems with your models and allows you to preview the end result, helping to further identify any other issues. Advanced users will need to decide if the premium features are worth paying for compared to open-source slicers.

In chapter V, we will be looking at a slicing software called Cura, and discuss all the settings you need for a high quality 3D print.

What are the materials used by the 3D printer?

The material used to print 3D objects on a 3D printer is known as filament. It is similar to ink for a 2d/desktop inkjet paper print. The material usually comes in a spool stocked in a spool holder of the printer with the base of the filament pushed in the extruder. 3D printers differ in terms of the level of compatibility of filaments. While some 3D printers are flexible enough to print different materials, some can only print the most commonly used PLA filament.

PLA, also known as polylactic acid or polylactide, is a thermoplastic made from renewable resources such as corn starch, tapioca roots or sugar cane. PLA has become a popular material because it is economically produced from renewable resources. Due to its more ecological origins, this material has become popular within the 3D printing industry. We have begun to see it in medical applications and food products

Another famous filament type is ABS, and it is used in the bodywork of cars, appliances, and mobile phone cases. It is a thermoplastic containing elastomers based on polybutadiene, making it more flexible and resistant to shocks. ABS filament is not biodegradable and shrinks in contact with air, so the printing platform must be heated.

In addition to PLA and ABS, we will discuss a few more filament types in chapter 4.

So till now, you have different bits of information/3D printing terminology floating in your mind. And since this book is going to concentrate on commercial-grade 3D printers which use FDM methodology, here is How it all comes together -

So if your desktop 2D paper printer needs paper and ink to print your pdf/ word doc., a 3D printer will need-

- STL file, which acts as your input like pdf or word file for your paper printer
- 3D slicer converts the STL file into G-Code, which are instructions for the 3D printer to lay down layers on the bed.
- Material called filament, equivalent to ink in your paper printer is heated to a temperature of around 200 degrees celsius used to print the 3D object.

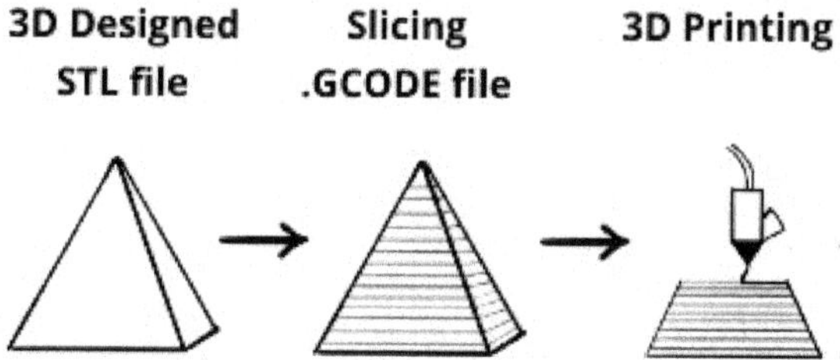

What are the other common 3D printing technologies?

In addition to FDM, which is going to be widely discussed in this book, here are some more common types of 3D printers

FDM(Fused Deposition Modeling) is the most common 3D printing method. A thin filament strand is fed into the printer and melted at the hotend (nozzle). The melted filament is laid onto a print bed, where it instantly solidifies. Subsequent layers are printed on top of each other until the model has finished. Materials used include PLA, ABS, etc. FDM 3D printers are the cheapest of all types in terms of hardware and running costs, which makes them the best kind of printer for educational purposes.

SLA(Stereolithography) involves using a light source to harden a liquid photopolymer. A build platform is submerged into a tub of liquid photopolymer resin, which acts as the material before a light source like lasers traces out an image on the resin to harden it. With FDM, one layer is applied at a time until the object is complete, in SLA compared to FDM the object created is highly detailed and accurate. However, the price tag of the material used and the printer are expensive compared to FDM printers.

SLS(Selective Laser Sintering) is a technology similar to SLA in that it uses a laser to trace over the material. Still, instead of a photopolymer resin, SLS 3D printers are filled with powered materials fused by laser. After the printing is done, models must be cleaned with compressed air. Now, if you are wondering what sintering is? Sintering is the act of using heat, compression, or a high-powered laser to make a powdered material fuse into a solid structure. SLS machines can produce high fidelity items, including precision, but they have high entry barriers. Machine and maintenance costs are expensive (among the most expensive compared to plastic printers), and they require skilled operators.

Is it possible to scan and print a real object? Like your favourite toy?

The short answer is Yes. You can use a technology called 3D scanning to create an STL file of your favourite toy at home. Just as 2D photos are made up of pixels, 3D scans are made up of tiny triangles or polygons. Polygons form a polygonal mesh, which replicates the object's geometry in minute detail and forms an STL file.

A 3D scanner which somewhat looks like a hair dryer, generates 3D scans. A scanner works like a video camera, which takes multiple shots of an object. A regular mobile camera, however, makes two-dimensional photographs. At the same time, the 3D scanner captures the geometry of the object's surface, and the photographs it has captured are worked into a 3D model rather than a video.

Now, the days of taking a selfie with your phone or going to a photo studio to take a family photo are gone. With the popularity of 3D scanning and 3D printing, you can now create a 3D selfie of yourself or the whole family on your bookshelf as long as the family can stand still in one place for a few minutes while the 3D scan is in progress.

On a serious note, 3D scanning is used in Archaeology and heritage preservation by scanning deteriorating museum artefacts and old ancient buildings. In the Art and Design fields, to create visually stunning special effects in movies, developing immersive, ultra-realistic VR applications.

Advanced 3D scanning technologies are becoming increasingly popular in forensics due to their portability, flexibility, and accuracy. Professional 3D scanning solutions are now being used around the world by police forces, multiple insurance companies, and even during court hearings for presenting evidence!

Where are the 3D printers being used today?

3D printers are being used in almost every field today because of the ease of rapid prototyping and reduced cost. Here are some areas to give you an idea -

Architecture, Architects can spend days creating physical models to explain their designs to clients. Using modern technology, they can use their existing CAD drawings to rapidly create a 3D model and 3D print. They save time, and complex geometries that can't be modelled by hand can be produced efficiently and at a low cost.

Automobiles, the automotive industry has been tapping the potential of 3D printing for decades already. 3D printing is instrumental in rapid prototyping and has significantly reduced design time and lead time on new car models. With 3D printing, custom jigs and other low volume parts can be created directly for the production line. Manufacturers can cut lead times by up to 90% and lower risk parts not fitting.

Dental, Combined with 3D scanning technologies, dentists can now 3D print moulds, visual aids, bridges, crowns, guards, etc. 3D printing eliminates the need for manual tasks, which saves time and money, as each product is accurately tailored to the patient.

Prosthetics, 3D printing can also change lives directly. There is a global shortage of prosthetics relative to demand. The time and financial cost required to acquire needed prosthetics can prove prohibitive, especially given the degree of customisation involved and the high need for prosthetic supplies. Prostheses and braces not built to specification can cause discomfort to those they should be assisting and empowering. In the case of children, in addition to a 3D printed prosthetic costing a fraction of the original cost, another one can be redesigned and scaled to fit as the child grows. Additionally, 3D printing allows the child to choose from a variety of colours and can also customise the prosthetic to symbolise their favourite superhero.

Jewellery, Creating 3D printed pieces that had a similar look and feel to traditionally handcrafted and cast jewellery used to be a challenge. However, following the latest round of advances in specialist high-end 3D modeling programs, and more printable materials on offer, more and more jewellery designers now prefer to 3D model and print their designs over traditional handcrafted methods.

The buying experience is made more tactile. As a result, clients can now try on prototypes of pieces they have helped design to ensure it looks and feels just right before purchasing. And the final designs can then be 3D printed and cast in a mould using the same workflow as traditional jewellery.

Spare & Replacements Parts The effects of losing or breaking parts of products or devices can range from the inconvenient to the disastrous. 3D printing will put behind the days of having to pay exorbitant repair costs or else throw away mostly functioning devices, by enabling consumers to produce replacement and spare parts. This can be as simple as creating a custom protective cover for an old smartphone, which you cannot find on any of the e-commerce sites, to creating a similar door handle for your bookshelf when the original one breaks.

Fashion and Smart Clothing One area in which the commercial and artistic potential of 3D printing will likely collide is in the field of fashion and smart clothing. As the pallet of materials and textiles usable in the 3D workflow increases, designers will be afforded an immense range of new possibilities.

Not only can 3D printing technology alter the production of textiles, but it will also provide the opportunity to create new textiles that are, for example, bulletproof, fireproof and capable of retaining heat. This particular branch of 3D workflow has yet to be perfected, but in the near future, we will see 3D printed clothing everywhere.

Medical field and Surgery, One of the key benefits of 3D printing is the ability to customise objects at no extra cost. The medical sector is taking advantage of this in various ways and one prominent field is that of hearing aids. The process begins by taking a 3D scan of the patient's ear, which ensures an accurate 3D print can be made that has a perfect fit for that specific patient. 3D printing has also made formerly impossible surgeries a reality. Replacing the upper jaw, forming a new skull and replacing cancerous vertebrae, all unthinkable before the advent of advanced 3D imaging and printing, have now been carried out successfully because of it.

Product Design, 3D printing enables product and industrial designers to develop prototypes within hours as opposed to weeks through traditional methods. The cost of creating a prototype is reduced to a small fraction of the cost, compared to traditional methods of tooling, mould making, etc.

Do you really need to buy a 3D printer?

A 3d printer won't transform you into a creative person. Although it may help the creative juices start flowing over time, it will let you transform those ideas into something tangible.

Once you get over the learning curve and are capable of producing quality prints that can be used for prototyping, repairing household items, and even making money (in some cases) by printing custom objects to sell to others. However, 3D printers can be a little expensive, as is the filament, you will need to learn to design the models and even troubleshoot the printer, which is covered in this book.

If you can't afford one directly, you will have to find a school/library or a maker space with a 3D printer. Or simply ask around. One of your old friends could own a 3D printer and would be happy to print your STL file for you and suggest improvements for your next design.

In addition, if you don't own a 3D printer, search for a 3D printing service, something along the lines of shapeways.com, robu.in, etc.

CHAPTER II

A quick history lesson: When was 3D printing invented?

This is a loaded question, with a lot of controversy surrounding who/when 3D printing was first invented. The 1980s were when 3D printing ideas became a reality. Unfortunately, the first half of the decade was filled with promising patents from investors that either ran out of money or were financed by groups that failed to see any commercial applications that could recoup their investment.

The first prominent patent of the decade was filed by Japanese inventor Dr. Hideo Kodama in 1981. He described his invention as a "rapid prototyping device". More importantly, he was the first person to ever apply for a patent that described a laser beam curing process. Sadly, his patent never went through as he abandoned financing the patent one year after filing it.

Next up was a trio of French inventors who came forward with a patent in 1984. Jean-Claude Andre, Olivier de Witte, and Alain le Mehaute were colleagues working for the French technology firm Alcatel and the French National Centre for Scientific Research. They followed Dr Kodama's focus on a "rapid prototyping device" to produce complex parts.

The first commercial 3D printer is generally attributed to Charles W. Hull and the Company 3D Systems in 1986. Mr Hull patented the term "stereolithography", which refers to making solid objects by "printing" thin layers of ultraviolet curable material one on top of another. By combining microprocessor control with the stereolithography process, Mr. Hull designed a machine that could be practical and inexpensive enough to be used outside of the research lab and inside commercial and higher education environments.

The technology most widely used in 3D printers to date, especially hobbyist and consumer-oriented models, is fused deposition modeling, a unique application of plastic extrusion, developed in 1988 by S. Scott Crump and commercialised by his Company Stratasys, which marketed its first FDM machine in 1992

The RepRap Project

Now comes the era when most people learned about 3D printing. Various events are responsible for this proliferation, starting with Z Corp. introducing a multicolour 3D printer in 2000. They repurposed the inkjet printing technology common to household full-colour printers, adapting it to print colourful 3D objects. While it hasn't evolved into an industry-standard, multicolour printing remains a popular fascination of some.

The following significant development came in 2004 with Adrian Bowyer starting the RepRap movement. His goal was to use 3D printers to manufacture more 3D printers, thus creating self-replicating machines. The 1.0 Darwin machine was the first practical application of RepRap's philosophy, and suddenly anyone had the power to make whatever they could dream up. Launched around the same time, Kickstarter gave home 3D printing another considerable boost as crowdfunded projects sprung up everywhere. Manufacturing was democratising fast.

The idea was a few years away from reality but quickly gained popularity in the 3D printing community, including Prusa Research founder Josef Pursa, who took the idea to the next level.

Marketplaces and virtual swap meets for trading, sharing, and acquiring designs sprung up everywhere, driving a massive groundswell of interest. When MakerBot arrived in 2009 with open-source Do-It-Yourself (DIY) kits to design and print just about anything, co-founder Bre Pettis became a superstar. It gave 3D printing the same cachet as past emerging technologies like social media, e-commerce, and even the Web. But what fun would that be if they couldn't exchange designs and print ideas? Well, that market gap was quickly filled by Thingiverse, which was launched in 2008.

Patents End – SLA, FDM and SLS in the public domain

In the early 2000s, Electronic hardware and software were at a point where 3D printing could have potentially been viable commercially. Still, Patents owned by multiple companies and individuals were a significant hindrance. The first patent to go was for SLA technology in 2009, the one Chuck Hull had filed to bring his SLA-1 printer to market.

Next to pass its best-before date was Stratasys' patent for FDM technology, ending in 2009. With these patents ending in 2009, competitors were quick to the market with new DIY printer kits. These kits were available at a far lower cost than before, ignoring the commercial, industrial market Stratasys had focused on. Instead, manufacturers aimed to connect with individual consumers and the burgeoning hobbyist community congregating online around Thingiverse, Objet, and Reprap technology.

The most notable DIY kit providers were BfB Rapman and Makerbot, both introducing their FDM products in 2009 shortly after the patent expirations.

It took a bit longer for SLA printers to attract hobbyist attention, but Formlabs was able to break through to this market in 2012 when they launched the first realistically affordable SLA printer for consumers, the Form 1, via a Kickstarter campaign.

The era of patents came to an end almost entirely in 2014 with the expirations of SLS patents. Now the technology of all three major forms of 3D printing is in the public domain, free to be experimented with and improved upon.

2008 saw the first 3D printed prosthetic limbs that could be printed as is, without requiring any further assembly after coming off the print bed. This development was celebrated by many and has helped improve countless lives with its accuracy, customization ability, and lower costs.

The trend of improving medicine continued in 2012, with the first prosthetic jaw being printed.

If someone were to quiz you on the dates, here is the year listing -

- 1981: First patent by Japanese Dr Hideo Kodama for Rapid prototyping device
- 1984: Stereolithography by 3 French engineers which was then abandoned
- 1986: Stereolithography was taken up by Charles W Hull
- 1988: First SLS machine by DTM Inc. then bought by 3D Systems
- 1992: FDM patent to Stratasys
- 2000: a 3D printed working kidney is created
- 2004: An open-source project is initiated (Reprap) by Adrian Bower
- 2008: The first 3D printed prosthetic leg
- 2009: The SLA and FDM patents expired, and these technologies were now in the public domain, which meant a lot of new companies emerged to sell commercial-grade 3D printers. Also, the launch of the MakerBot 3D printer, which was the first commercial-grade printer.
- 2012: The first prosthetic jaw being printed.

Today, additive manufacturing is a mature technology. The consumer interest and robustness of industrial platforms grew throughout the 2010s as the MakerBot hype settled down and the industry found a groove. Some think additives will replace traditional CNC and milling manufacturing in the future.

CHAPTER III

Parts of a 3D Printer

As 3D printers become more and more popular and the cost of entry in 3D printing reduces, most folks prefer to buy a fully assembled machine, while few like to explore a little more with DIY kit 3D printers. While working with DIY machines, the most exciting part is exploring the different 3D printer parts that make it such a powerful technology. Though it can get complicated at times to complete the assembly in a few hours, the experience does provide a lot of know-how about the 3D printer anatomy. By learning about the parts, one gets a better understanding of the working of 3D printers. Hence, you can utilise the knowledge later when printing with the machine. In addition, you can even solve minor to major problems such as a nozzle jam and many others, when familiar with the inside out of these 3D printers.

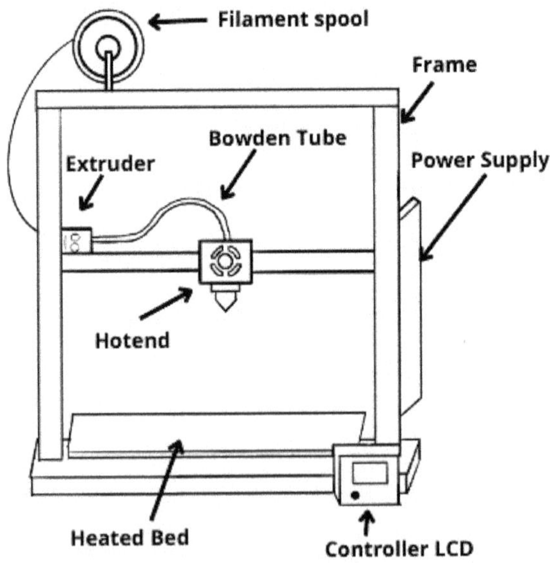

Here is the list of the major parts that make up a 3D printer

Frame

Helps keep all the other components of your 3D printer together in one place. It also maintains the stability of the entire machine. If your frame is robust, you will have a more durable 3D printer.

3D printer manufacturers use different materials, and the most common ones are metal and acrylic. In the old days, when we got our first 3D printer DIY kit, it was made of wooden frames. However, to maintain the highest stability, one must choose the metal body.

In addition, open and closed frame designs also make a difference. A closed frame offers better results by maintaining consistent temperature around the print space, but these can be expensive. Few printers also offer semi-enclosed frames, which can be a good compromise for the price.

Power Supply

Helps in supplying power for a smooth operation of a 3D printer. You can find the power supply mounted on the frame, or it can also be available separately along with another controller box. However, the mounted one provides a compact look and occupies less space.

MotherBoard

Also called the Controller board. If the power supply is the heart of the 3D printer, then the motherboard is the brain responsible for maintaining the smooth processing of the machine. Controller boards handle all the logic behind 3D printing, such as parsing G-code (tells your printer what/how to print) files, regulating temperature, and controlling motion. The latter is particularly important if we're talking about FDM and stepper motors.

Controller LCD

This is how the user controls the printer. Through the knob, the user can go home, to bring the printer head to the X, Y and Z axis to the 0th

position. And also move the axis, preheat components, start/stop/pause prints, and much more. Hence, these machines can work as standalone machines, compared to the past when you had to have a computer connected to the USB port of the printer to execute the commands.

USB and SD Card Slot

USB and SD card slot are extensions of the MotherBoard, used as an interface for feeding G-code to the printer. You can upload a file to a micro SD card and insert it into the printer or print directly from a computer via the USB port. However, many new 3D printers are now available with a Wi-Fi setup.

Heated Bed

Is the component on which the print is created. The filaments are deposited on the heated bed, one layer at a time to build the entire object. You can find heated as well as non-heated print beds. A non-heated print bed may be enough for PLA. However, for advanced filaments, heated beds are recommended. This helps enhance adhesion and stability for the first layer of the print.

The print beds are designed using different materials, for example, aluminium and glass print beds. Some 3D printers offer automatic calibration of print beds. However, in the 3D printer DIY kits, you will need to level the bed manually using a sheet of paper. Usually, there are four levelling screws located under the four corners of the heated bed. They are used to adjust and level the bed.

In addition, some beds come with removable build plates on top, which are semi-flexible and remove larger prints easily.

HotEnd

Is exactly as it sounds and is the component that melts the filament and where it is extruded from. This is made of a few components, as you must have guessed by looking at the diagram on the next page. You will need components to measure the temperature and cool it down if it gets too hot.

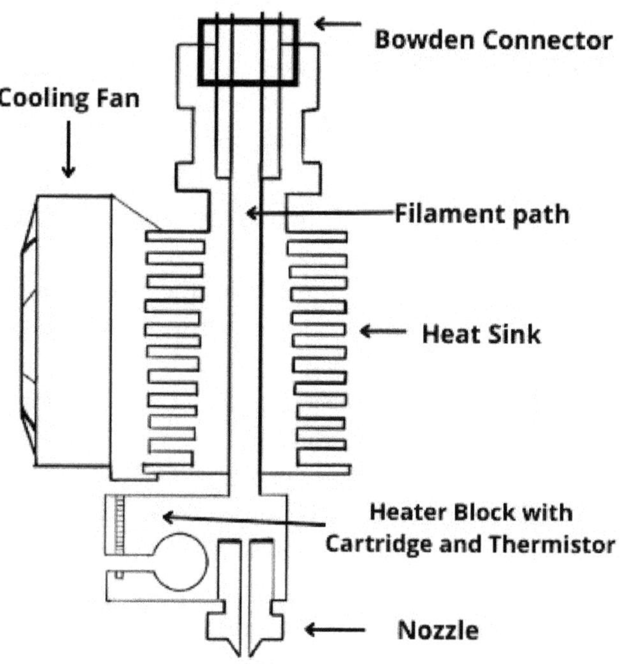

Bowden connector, this component holds the end of the Bowden tube inside the hotend.

Heat Sink, the hotend fan blows on here to keep the upper part of the hotend cool.

Hotend Cooling Fan, this Fan cools the heat sink of the hotend

Heater Block is the part that is heated by the heater cartridge, houses the thermistor as well

Heater Cartridge, heating component of the hotend

Thermistor reads the temperature of the hotend

Nozzle extrudes the melted plastic.

Part Cooling Fan, this fan cools the filament as it is extruded and helps to improve bridging and layer adhesion

Motion Controller

As the 3D printers work along three axis, X, Y, and Z, the motion controller receives instructions from the motherboard. The signals for movement from the motherboard are sent to the stepper motor, which with the help of the belts mounted on them, moves the other components like the Bed and Hot end. Here is a brief description of the components that govern the motion of the 3D printer -

Stepper Motors: These are responsible for the mechanical movement of the device and are controlled by a Stepper driver, which is a mini circuit board mounted on the motherboard. Today, these come integrated with the motherboard. These motors connect with X, Y as well as the Z axis. These motors help in driving the print head and print bed. Because the rotations are made in steps, they are called Stepper motors.

Belts: The belts connected to the stepper motors are responsible for moving X axis and Y axis. The movement happens from side to side. This movement does affect the print speed and precision. Hence is very crucial to attaining best results. You need to ensure that the belts aren't loose so that the print quality is not impacted. You can use the screws on the tensioners to loosen or tighten the belt.

Threaded rods: Threaded rods are connected to stepper motors. The print head moves in upward and downward directions with the movement of threaded rods. In a few 3D printers, the print bed movement relies on Threaded rods. So, the Z axis movement is dependent on Threaded rods.

End Stops: End stops ensure that the endpoints are marked along the three axis when the movement of components takes place. It is usually a mechanical on and off switch.

Extruder

Is the part of the 3D printer responsible for pushing the filament along to the Hotend, and a stepper motor controls the pushing of the filament. A 3D printer extruder comprises many different components that do a combination of jobs. They include -

Extruder Stepper Motor, the motherboard sends a signal to the stepper motor to extrude the filament, which governs how much filament will be pushed through the hotend.

Extruder Gear digs into filament to extrude it and is attached to the stepper motor.

Extruder Bearing presses filament against extruder gear, helps with smooth extrusion.

Lever, this needs to be pressed when you want to load and unload filament, which increases the tension on the tension spring. Thereby, increasing the distance between the extruder gear and bearing releasing the filament.

There are two main types of extruders that you will find on commercial-grade 3D printers, Direct and Bowden.

Direct extruder

The filament runs from the filament spool to the coldend, which is the combination of extruder stepper motor and extruder bearing, to the hotend, all in one piece. This means the drive and the gear that moves the filament along are directly above and attached to the hotend. Because the extruder sits directly on top of the hotend, the extruder itself is heavier and slower. However, many prefer this as printing flexible 3D filaments using a direct extruder, is easier. The filament has less distance to travel with a direct extruder before getting melted and deposited. Consequently, there's less opportunity for issues during the extrusion process.

Bowden Extruder

The cold end and the hotend are separated by a tube (also called the Bowden tube), where the filament runs along. As opposed to a direct extruder, a Bowden extruder is much lighter and faster because the only moving part is the hotend. The coldend, with the drive, is positioned on a fixed point on the printer.

Bowden extruders print high-quality models and are great for printing models that feature long, continuous designs.

Some 3D printers are equipped with dual extruders as well. One can print simultaneously with two different colour filaments with a dual extruder.

CHAPTER IV

What are the input materials used with a 3D Printer?

In the case of your 2D paper Inkjet printers, the input material used is black ink and a colour ink cartridge, but in the case of a 3D printer, since you are building a 3D object, the material used is called a filament spool. The filament spool contains a 1.75 mm(millimetres) or 3 mm filament wire, which is wound around the spool holder, which is circular in size and mostly made of plastic or cardboard.

The world of 3D filaments is a vast one. So, if you're going to use these materials for your project, you must know about your fundamental options. These are some of the different types of 3D printing filaments and the benefits each can bring to your finished product.

PLA (Poly Lactic Acid)

PLA filaments are among the most popular 3D materials. They're durable and easier to print than other varieties. It's important to note that PLA has a lower printing temperature, protecting it from shrinking or warping during printing. PLA's flexibility is generally low. It isn't recommended for items meant to bend/flex.

PLA is a biodegradable thermoplastic filament derived from renewable resources like cornstarch, sugar cane, tapioca roots, and potato starch. It is the most environment-friendly compared to other filaments mentioned below. Due to this and its low-toxicity features, hobbyists prefer this filament over the others.

- Print Temperature Range: 180 – 230 °C (this will be mentioned on the Filament box you buy or on the manufacturer's website.)
- Strength: High | Flexibility: Low | Durability: Medium
- Shrinkage/warping: Minimal
- Print bed temperature: 20 – 60 °C (but not needed)

ABS (Acrylonitrile Butadiene Styrene)

ABS was the most popular or commonly used 3D printer filament before PLA took over the spot. It is used in various applications because it is tough and high impact-resistant.

ABS is the best 3D printer filament for moving parts, automotive parts, electronic housing, and toys. ABS filament is also used in pipes, automotive components, electronic assemblies, protective headgear like bicycle helmets, music instruments, kitchen appliances, LEGO bricks, etc.

Printing with ABS also produces unpleasant fumes that can irritate some people. Good ventilation is essential. Combined, these things make ABS a material favoured more by professionals than amateur users.

- Print Temperature Range: 210 – 260 °C
- Strength: High | Flexibility: Medium | Durability: High
- Shrinkage/warping: Considerable (for a large part, you will observe warping of the edges of the print, which means you will need a higher bed temperature.)
- Print bed temperature: 80 – 100 °C

PETG (Poly Ethylene Terephthalate Glycol)

If PLA is the most popular filament, PETG is in the running for second place. It rivals PLA in terms of strength and durability and is a great general-use material for crafting ideal models. PETG is notably more flexible than PLA, making it a better fit for printing functional objects. PETG filament is best for printing products subject to sudden or sustained stress like protective components, such as, cell phone cases and mechanical parts. It is also food-safe, so it's suitable for cups, plates, and water or food containers.

PETG is hygroscopic, meaning it absorbs moisture from the air. This hurts the printability of the material, so make sure to store the 3D printer filament in a cool, dry place and, if necessary, dry it before use. PETG is sticky when printed, making this 3D printer filament a poor choice for support structures but good for layer adhesion.

- Print Temperature Range: 210 – 250 °C
- Strength: High | Flexibility: Medium | Durability: High

- Shrinkage/warping: Minimal
- Print bed temperature: 40 – 70 °C

TPU (Thermoplastic Polyurethane)

TPU is perfect for items with superior durability and flexibility. This material leans more rigid when raw, which makes it easier to print on most printers. But, once crafted, it's very soft and stretchable, allowing it to hold up against physical stress. Its rubber-like texture also helps it maintain its elasticity in colder temperatures.

Due to its high flexibility, TPU is ideal for objects like toys, novelty items, wearables, phone cases, and visual products.

- Print Temperature Range: 210 – 240 °C
- Strength: Medium(Stretchable) | Flexibility: Very High | Durability: High
- Shrinkage/warping: Minimal
- Print bed temperature: 40 – 60 °C

Nylon

Nylon acts as a durable base and combines well with various materials, including glass, carbon fiber, and Kevlar. As a result, these materials have a diverse range of uses that cover several different industrial and crafting industries. Nylon offers quality strength and flexibility, which further expands the creative endeavours in which it can be used. The engineering grade of Nylon is ideal for machine parts, mechanical components, structural parts, gears and bearings, dynamic load, containers, tools, consumer products, and toys.

Now, since it is Nylon, you can dye it before or after the printing process. But like PETG, it is hygroscopic, meaning it absorbs moisture, so remember to store it in a cool, dry place to keep the filament in prime condition, ensuring better quality prints.

- Print Temperature Range: 240 – 270 °C
- Strength: High| Flexibility: Very High | Durability: High
- Shrinkage/warping: Considerable

- Print bed temperature: 80– 100 °C

Carbon fiber

Carbon fiber filaments are a great option if you're looking for something lightweight. They're strong and durable, so they're great for functional products—particularly sports equipment. However, its rough texture has the potential to damage incompatible 3D printers. So, double-check your printer's capabilities before purchasing this material. To print Carbon fiber you will need a special nozzle, or you should have a couple of extra nozzles handy in your kit so that you can replace the existing nozzle if it corrodes and the diameter increases considerably.

Carbon fiber parts are stiffer than PLA, with better dimensional stability for warp-free printing, and excellent layer adhesion.

- Print Temperature Range: 195 – 220 °C
- Strength: Very High| Flexibility: Low | Durability: High
- Shrinkage/warping: Minimal
- Print bed temperature: 40 – 70 °C

Wood

The filament contains a mixture of recycled wood with a binding polymer. Thus, helping you produce a 3D object that looks and smells like wood. Due to its wooden nature, it's difficult to tell that the object is 3D printed. So, if you want to achieve that wooden appearance, using wood filament is similar to using a thermoplastic filament like PLA. There are many wood filament varieties available today, such as Pine, Birch, Cedar, Ebony, and Willow. Still, the range also extends to less common types, like Bamboo, Cherry, Coconut, Cork, and Olive.

Wood filament is used to create figurines, and awards, which can be varnished and oiled. In this case, the aesthetic and tactile appeal comes at the cost of reduced flexibility and strength. The part is not as strong as a milled natural wood part.

- Print Temperature Range: 195 – 210 °C

- Strength: Medium| Flexibility: Medium | Durability: Low(when compared to the exact part made of natural wood)
- Shrinkage/warping: Minimal
- Print bed temperature: 40 – 50 °C

Metal filled

Like wood-filled 3D printer filament, the metal-filled filament isn't entirely made from metal. It's a mix of metal powder and either PLA or ABS. But that doesn't stop the print from having the look and feel of metal, even if the weight is metal-like.

Bronze, brass, copper, aluminium, and stainless steel are just a few of the varieties of metal 3D printer filaments commercially available. And if there's a specific look you're interested in, don't be afraid to polish, weather, or tarnish your metal items after printing. A little post-processing can go a long way in giving the part an antique look.

Like carbon fiber filament, you may need to replace your nozzle a little sooner due to printing with metal, as the grains are somewhat abrasive, resulting in increased nozzle wear.

- Print Temperature Range: 195 – 230 °C
- Strength: Very High| Flexibility: Low | Durability: Low(when compared to the exact part made of metal)
- Shrinkage/warping: Minimal
- Print bed temperature: 40 – 50 °C

Conductive

The filament that does as its name implies conducts electricity. With the addition of conductive carbon particulates to PLA or ABS, it's easy to actualise hobbyist projects by printing low-voltage electronic circuits. To couple this filament with a regular PLA/ABS project, you will need a 3D printer with dual extruders. If you can't find one in your locale, you can also buy a 3D pen to extrude conductive filament in your PLA/ABS part. Try coupling a circuit board with LEDs, sensors, or even a Raspberry Pi or Arduino if you're experimenting.

- Print Temperature Range: 195 – 220 °C
- Strength: High| Flexibility: Medium | Durability: Medium(usually, this filament is used in combination with regular PLA/ABS so that these parameters will depend on the PLA/ABS parameters)
- Shrinkage/warping: Minimal
- Print bed temperature: Not applicable as bed temperature will be governed by the filament used for the base part, which can be PLA or ABS.

PVA (Polyvinyl alcohol)

PVA is soluble in water and that's precisely what commercial applications take advantage of. The most popular uses include packaging for dishwasher detergent pods. PVA is a great support material when paired with another 3D printer filament in a dual extrusion 3D printer, specifically if you are printing a part with complex geometry. Dry boxes and silica pouches are a must if you plan to keep a spool of PVA usable in the long run.

This material is also the best filament for freshwater sports fishing, where PVA bags filled with bait are thrown into the water. The bag rapidly dissolves and releases the bait to attract the fish.

- Print Temperature Range: 190 – 230 °C
- Strength: Medium| Flexibility: Medium | Durability: Low(this filament is meant to dissolve with water)
- Shrinkage/warping: Minimal
- Print bed temperature: 40 – 60 °C

In addition, there are many more exotic filaments like Glow in the Dark, Magnetic, Ceramic, poly-carbonate, etc. There are a couple of new ones released every year.

CHAPTER V

How to slice a 3D object?

A common difference between a successful and a failed 3D print could be the appropriate 3D slicer settings. So that means, whether you work on a desktop 3D printer or a commercial one, proper slicer settings ought to be known by every user.

What Is a 3D Slicer?

A 3D slicer is a 3D printing software that takes note of a digital 3D model to be printed and converts it to directives for the 3D printer to create an object. The slicer may cut your 3D model into various horizontal layers as per its settings. And it even calculates the amount of printing material and the time required to print the object. But, the choice of the slicer setting depends on the desired result of the 3D material/ filament used. Almost all of this information is pushed into your 3D printer in the form of a G-Code file.

What is a G-Code file?

Almost all desktop 3D printers use a numerically controlled programming language made up of a series of commands called G-Code. Most of these commands start with a G, so the name “G-Code file”, but there are also some common machine-specific codes that start with an M. These commands tell your printer exactly what actions to perform – where to move, what speed to use, what temperatures to set, and much more.

Here is a sample snippet from the G-Code file

- *G28 - home all axis to X=0, Y=0, and Z=0*
- *G1 X0 Y0 F2000 - move to the X=0 Y=0 position on the bed at a speed of 2000 mm/min*
- *G1 Z20 F1200 - move the Z-axis to Z=20mm at a slower speed of 1200 mm/ min*
- *M104 S210 T0 - start heating T0 hotend to 210* °C

- *M106 S255 - set the parts fan to full speed*
- *M140 S50 - start heating the bed to 50* °C

If the above is confusing, there is nothing to worry about, as the generation of the file is automatically done by the 3D slicer software. You just need to upload the G-Code to the SD card of your 3D printer.

If you're new to 3D printing, the best slicer to get started is Cura, as it is easy to use. It has 3D printer profiles and suggested slicer settings for famous commercial available 3D printers like the Ender 3. Once you have installed Cura, you will have to go to the Add printer section and select your printer. We will use the Ender 3 standard profile for the remainder of this chapter. In addition, we will consider PLA filament as this is the likely filament you are going to get started with.

These are some primary 3D slicer settings you should know before starting your 3D printing journey.

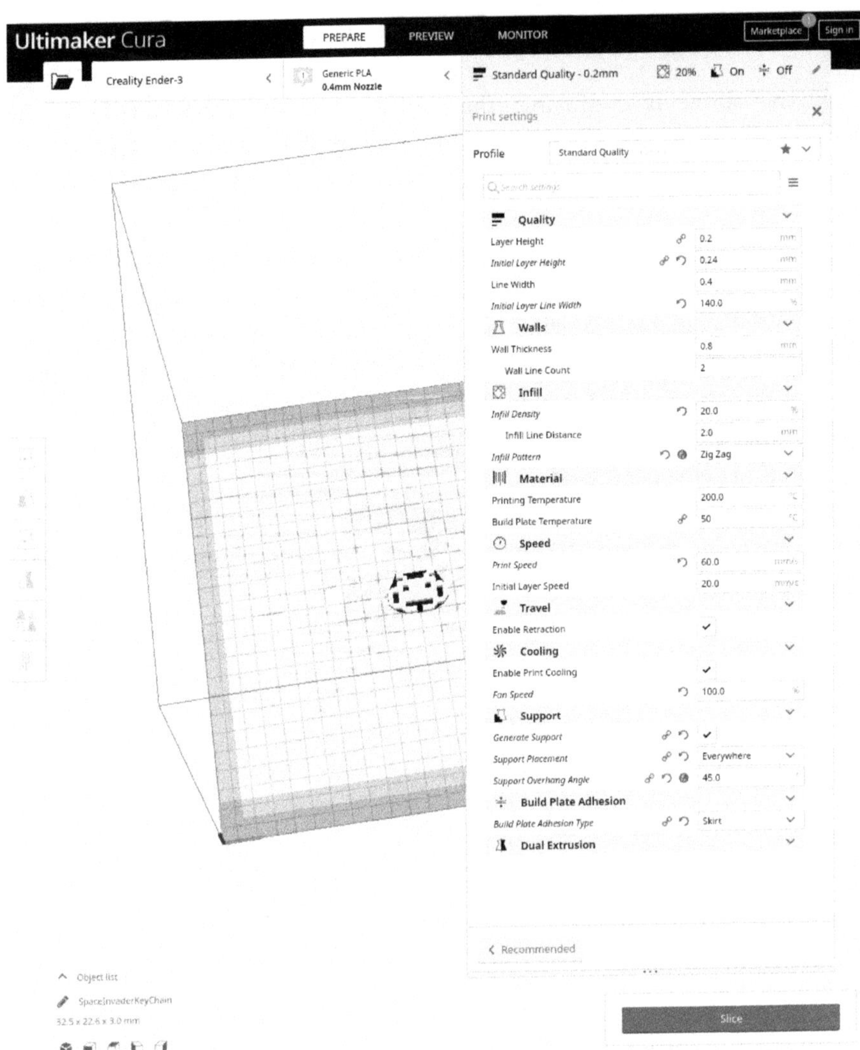

Cura Slicer Settings

Quality - Layer height governs the final look/resolution

Layer height could almost be synonymous with the resolution of the print. It denotes the height of each layer of filament deposited by a printer to form a complete object. If you halve the layer height, the print resolution is doubled. This means that you get twice as many layers in one print. Another way of saying the same thing is, if an object is made of thinner layers, it will have a smoother surface and would require the least post-processing after 3D printing. However, these take more time to be completed since the number of layers deposited is more. The objects printed with thicker layers will be printed faster but with print layers visible distinctly and the surfaces rougher. They may need a good amount of post-processing after being entirely printed and dried.

Since we are using the Ender 3, here are the possible values: 0.08, 0.12, 0.16, 0.20,0.24 mm.... The values are in multiples of 0.04, as the printer raises the hotend with the Z-axis motor by 0.04 mm per step. So for a standard quality print, you would use a value of layer height as 0.2 mm, but if you are printing a test model, you increase the layer height to 0.28 mm, which would give you a lower quality model, but the print time would be less.

Observe, the Initial **Layer Height** parameter is set to 0.24 mm. This is done so that a thicker initial layer on your print bed gives better adhesion to the 3D object. Basically, the 3D print object sticks better to the print bed.

Line width parameter gives the width of the line laid by the printer nozzle. Usually, the line width is set as the nozzle width, which is 0.4mm.

Initial Layer Line Width is a percentage value and is usually set to higher than 100% so that the initial layer line width is slightly bigger, so the 3D print object sticks better to the print bed.

Wall Thickness – Strength of printed object

Wall thickness is one of the significant factors affecting the strength of the 3D object and denotes the thickness of the side walls. It is defined as 'the number of times a 3D printer traces the outer walls of a design before going to the hollow inner section of the same. Wall thickness is preset to 0.8 mm in almost all kinds of 3D printers. However, if you intend to create a highly durable, water-proof print, you can always increase the shell thickness.

Wall line Count parameter is calculated automatically. If your nozzle width is 0.4 mm and wall thickness is 0.8 mm, the hotend will have to place two layers to build the wall.

Infill Density – another parameter important for Strength

The space density inside an object's outer shell is known as Infill. It is generally measured as a percentage instead of mm. The object tends to be stronger, heavier and more time-consuming to be built when the infill is a higher percentage. Therefore, it is not wise to print with 100% infill every time since this is more expensive in terms of taking more time and material.

If you plan to 3D print a snowman without any infill that is 0%, the snowman will collapse and break if you sequence it. So, for an item for display on your bookshelf, it is recommended to have an infill of 15 to 20%. And the more sturdy ones, for example, a hook printing to hold a heavy painting, can go for anything between 75 to 100 % of the infill.

Infill Line distance is the distance between the infill lines. This is calculated automatically. If the infill density is changed from 20% to 40%, the line distance changes from 6 mm to 3 mm.

Infill patterns: There are numerous infill patterns that govern integrity, quality, and strength. Choosing an infill pattern all depends on where your 3D print is going to be used. If your print is a display item on your bookshelf, use something simple like "Zig-zag" infill. But, if you need something mechanically robust, use Tri-Hexagon.

Material Temperature and why it counts

If not properly adjusted, it can lead to over-extrusion and blobs. For a smooth extrusion of PLA filaments, at least 190 °C is required. An over-extrusion is likely to take place at 220 °C. It is not worth setting the temperature too low or too high.

For the material temperature, check the box in which your filament came in. It should mention a temperature range to use. Or check the manufacturer's website.

Build Plate Temperature. This is the temperature used for the printer bed. For PLA, you don't need a heated bed/build plate. But if you have a printer like the Ender 3 that comes with a heated build plate, keep the temperature around 50 °C so that your part sticks to the bed. For material like ABS, a build plate temperature of more than 70 °C is critical because the part will tend to warp. That is, the edges of the part come off the bed.

Speed, how to set the print speed.

Print speed refers to the rate at which the extruder travels and lays down the 3D printing material. In addition, print speed will always depend on several factors such as the kind of 3D printer used, the filament used, the design you print and the layer height, etc.

The challenge here is to balance print quality with how much time the 3D object takes to complete. Keep in mind that you will have to expect a loss in terms of quality with increasing speed. If the hot end moves slower, it will be able to work with more detail. However, it is vital to keep an eye out that the print speed is not set too slow. After all, you will not want to wait several weeks for the print to complete.

The average speed of Ender 3 has proven to be between 45 and 65 mm/s. But, if you plan to print a flexible material like TPU, you will have to drop the speed to 30 mm/s.

Initial layer speed, as a suggestion, keep your initial layer speed as slow as 20 mm/s. This will help the print stick to the bed.

Travel, the role of Retraction

If the 3D object has discontinuous surfaces, the retraction feature informs the 3D printer to stop extruding material from the nozzle and extrude it only where required. Usually, retraction is always enabled in your 3D printer.

Cooling

Enabling the print cooling option, starts the print cooling fan, which is part of the hotend setup. The fan improves the quality of layers with short layer times. You can experiment with Fan speed based on the climate condition of the room in which your 3D printer is placed.

Support, preventing your uneven objects from failures

Supports are used on surfaces of the object which have nothing or not enough base material. For instance, while the objects are printed in layers, the part that extends above 45 degrees will have no first layer of the filament and may be printed as an overhang. These overhangs can lead to droops and you need a support object to get printed below to get the desired 3D object.

For example, if you are printing a human bust with both hands horizontally, you will need to check the checkbox for the Generate support option to add loose material under the hands, which can be removed once the print is complete.

Build Plate Adhesion so that the object sticks to the bed

If the printed objects start to warp at the bottom, this could lead to the prints not sticking on the print bed, causing a failure. For best platform adhesion, here are two major settings which you can try

Raft is a horizontal grid formed under the object to be printed and acts as a platform for the object to stick on the build platform.

Brim these are the lines around the bottom of the print, similar to the brim of hats, which keep the object stuck well to the surface without leaving any marks.

This option is used in case we have a 3D object with a lot of surface at the bottom, like a cube, and we need a line printed around the model just so that the extrude can start oozing out some filament.

With the above settings, you should have no problems when 3D printing simple 3D models. Using the default profile setting, you will need to do some experimentation before finding the option that's right for your printer and the 3D model you are trying to print. Ideally, slicer settings don't have to be changed if you are printing similar models and the same filament. But if you try a model with complex geometry and it fails, try reducing the print speed by 30% and also use Raft for the Build plate adhesion parameter.

With Slicer, the idea is to keep changing the parameters of a few things until you find the correct value for you.

CHAPTER VI

Your first print: step by step instructions

This chapter will serve as a revision of the previous four chapters. And will take you through the steps you need to follow once you have unboxed your printer to print your first object successfully. For the unboxing and assembling of the 3D printer, just in case you bought a kit, I am sure you will be able to figure it out by watching a couple of youtube videos.

Step 1: Heat your Hotend and load the filament.

To 3D print an object, you first need to decide on a filament you will use, for example, PLA, ABS etc., as described in chapter IV. If you plan on using PLA, check your filament box for the recommended temperature. If not mentioned, set 200 °C as your Hotend temperature. In the case of Ender 3, the control unit with the LCD screen and the circular dial will have an option called Preheat PLA.

Once you see the Hotend reach 200 °C on the LCD, load the filament by pressing the extruder lever and push the filament into the Bowden tube and ensure that you see the filament oozing as a thin string from the extruder. In addition, the motion menu on your LCD screen should have an option to extrude filament automatically. In this case, once you give the command to extrude 15mm of filament, you should see the extruder gear move to push the filament into your Bowden tube, causing the filament to ooze out from the nozzle. This means your Extruder and Hotend are functioning as desired.

Step 2: Prepare the Print Bed

Ensure that your 3D print sticks to the bed. You can use blue painter's tape for PLA, and if you have a glass bed for your printer, you can use hairspray for ABS prints.

In case your 3D print does not stick to the bed and you don't have a heated bed, you can also try glue sticks that you get at your local stationery shop. But, if you are using an Ender 3, we have a heated bed. And the printer also comes with the removable top sheet on the bed, which means you directly print on the Bed.

Step 3: Home your 3D printer Hotend and level your Bed

Levelling the bed and setting the nozzle will improve the quality of your 3D print. To make this easier, you can use a sheet of paper(regular paper from your 2D inkjet printer) to determine the distance between the nozzle and the bed.

Home the Hotend, using the motion menu on the LCD screen. This means your hotend will go to X=0, Y=0 and Z=0. Ensure that the nozzle is clean and at an appropriate distance from the bed, then insert paper under the model. If the paper does not go under the nozzle, you will have to rotate the knobs just below your bed to bring the bed down. Keep turning your knob down until the paper passes through between the hotend and the bed.

Once done, pull the bed in front so that the hotend is at the back of the printer. In the case of an Ender 3, you will have to disable the stepper using the LCD menu to move the Bed. Follow the same process in the paragraph above, till the paper just passes through, between the Hotend and the bed. This has to be repeated to all four corners and the centre of the bed.

Step 4: Download a simple STL from the Internet

If you are new to 3D printing for your first print, instead of designing something from scratch, 3D print a famous STL file that has been 3D printed by other folks with a 3D printer. For this, you can download a simple STL file from the internet, using the website that hosts 3D models like -

- Thingiverse.com
- Yeggi.com
- MyMinifactory.com

While selecting a file, choose something with a good base and nothing hanging from it, like a keychain with your favourite superhero logo.

Step 5: Slice the STL file

Getting the slicer setting right for your 3D model is critical and can be the difference between a successful and failed 3D print. The slicer cuts the 3D model into various horizontal layers, and the resolution and smoothness of your print can depend on slicer settings like Layer Height, Print Temperature, and Retraction. The strength is governed by settings like Wall thickness and Infill.

For the Ender 3, here is a good starting point for Cura slicer settings for PLA filament.

- Layer height: 0.2 mm
- Wall Thickness: 0.8 mm
- Printing speed: 60 mm/s
- Speed of the first layer: 20 mm/s
- Enable Retraction: Yes
- Enable Cooling: Yes, with Fan Speed as 100%
- Print temperature: 200 °C
- Printing bed temperature: 50 °C
- Infill: 20%
- Infill Pattern: Zig Zag
- Build Plate Adhesion Type: Skirt

Now load your 3D model STL in your slicer and click the Slice button to generate the G-Code file.

Step 6: 3D print the G-Code file

Copy the G-Code file created by the Slicer into an SD card. Insert the SD card and use the Ender 3 LCD and knob to select the G-Code file and start the Print.

Now, keep an eye out to check that the skirt and the first layer of filament have good bed adhesion. Move your finger across the skirt to check that it is not peeling off the bed. If it does, stop your print, and level the bed again. Basically, you will have to turn the knobs slightly to bring the bed marginally higher.

Once you are done with the first print, you observe that you have good bed adhesion. Try printing the 3D Benchy by CreativeTools from Thingiverse, which is a small boat(https://www.thingiverse.com/thing:763622).

3D Benchy is a 3D model designed for testing and benchmarking 3D printers. It is a small recognisable object that you can download for free.

It is intended to 3D-print quickly and be a fun tool for calibrating your 3D printer. If this is printed smoothly and the finish of the final object is smooth, you can consider your 3D printer fully functional and calibrated.

Step 7: Post-processing

Your first 3D print is something simple, so you will not need any post-processing. But if you want to go overboard, you always try applying epoxy to the 3D part to give a smooth textured finish.

Say in the future, you plan to use a wood filament to print a figurine and want to give it an antique look, you could sand, varnish and even oil the part.

In addition, if you want to print something large, like the bust of Buddha, you will have to cut your STL file into multiple parts, 3D print them individually and then stick them with glue, or use a 3D pen with the same filament. Finally, for the smooth finish, do a little bit of sanding.

CHAPTER VII

3D design: Learning to use Tinkercad

Tinkercad is the go-to 3D design software for anyone looking to delve into 3D modeling. It gives you the foundational knowledge to progress to more advanced 3D Design software like Fusion 360 and Sketchup mentioned in Chapter I.

The term TinkerCAD already contains the abbreviation CAD, which stands for Computer-Aided Design. The platform offers an intuitive and simple web-based platform for creating 3D models, which means no software needs to be installed on your computer. You just need the latest version of the internet browser, like Chrome. All projects created are stored in the Cloud servers so that you can access your design anywhere, from home to school or even your local coffee shop with WiFi.

With Tinkercad, you can, not only design and create 3D objects, but the platform also offers you the possibility to deal with electronic circuits and code blocks.

So let's get started with our 3D design journey. As part of the hands-on, we will discuss creating a keychain, Phone holder and more. And for more tutorials, go to https://goanfpv.in/3DPrintingBook

Create an account

Before we start 3D designing, you will have to create an account on Tinkercad website. Go to https://www.tinkercad.com/, and on the top right-hand corner, click the Join Now button, then select create a personal account. Use your email, Google account or Apple account to create a user on the website.

Once you are on the home page, you will find your account name on the left. You can click on it and upload your photo, which is optional. So if you are eager to get started, click the Create new design button.

Tinkercad workspace overview

Once you click on the Create a new design button, the workspace for creating and modifying 3D objects opens.

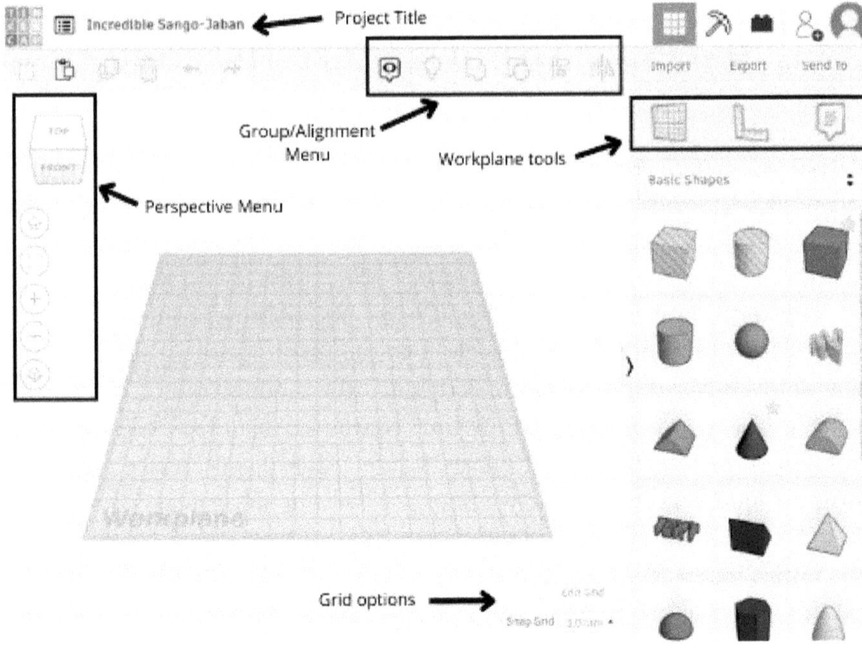

Workplane

The light blue grid at the centre is called the workplane, where you will build 3D models. Think of this as your worktable where you place your models to work on them. With the help of your computer mouse scroll, you can Zoom in and Zoom out.

To look around your workplane in 3D dimensional space, press and hold the right click of your mouse and move your mouse pointer. And, if you press and hold your scroll wheel and move your mouse left or right, the plane can be dragged in 2D space.

Project title

In the top left corner is the name of your project. Tinkercad, by default, assigns the project a name like Incredible Sango-Jaban. But you can click on it to rename it to something meaningful, something like Keychain.

Perspective Menu

In the area on the left upper side, vertically, is the Perspective menu, which allows looking at your 3D object from all angles, Zoom In/Out.

The small cube allows you to turn the view, to suit your viewing angle. Simply click on the cube with the mouse left button and move the mouse to rotate. Or if you want to specifically view the 3D models, Top, Bottom, Back, Front, Left, Right-click on the cube.

Below the cube, there is a small house-like icon called Home View. If you get lost with all the movement of your 3D workplane, you can come back to the original home view by clicking the Home View icon.

With the rectangle icon below, you can fit/look at all objects placed on the workplane at the same time.

The + and – signs are for zooming in and zooming out.

And the last icon allows you to switch between orthographic and perspective views.

Copy/Paste Menu

Just above the Perspective menu, there are options to Copy, Paste, Duplicate and Delete. To use these, you will have to first select a shape/object. You can also choose multiple shapes/objects by a rectangular selection window with the left click of your mouse. You also have undo and redo arrows, but you should try and use ctrl+z for undo and ctrl+y for redo on your keyboard.

Shapes and Symbols

To create an object, you can work with already existing objects. Simple objects can be found in the - Basic Shapes drop-down menu. To place an object like the red cube on the workplane, simply click on the object and move it to the workplane. If you click on the small star in the upper-right corner, the shape will be assigned to your favourites.

Once you place the cube on the workplane, the setting for the object will open. Try changing each of these parameters individually to see how the object's shape and size change.

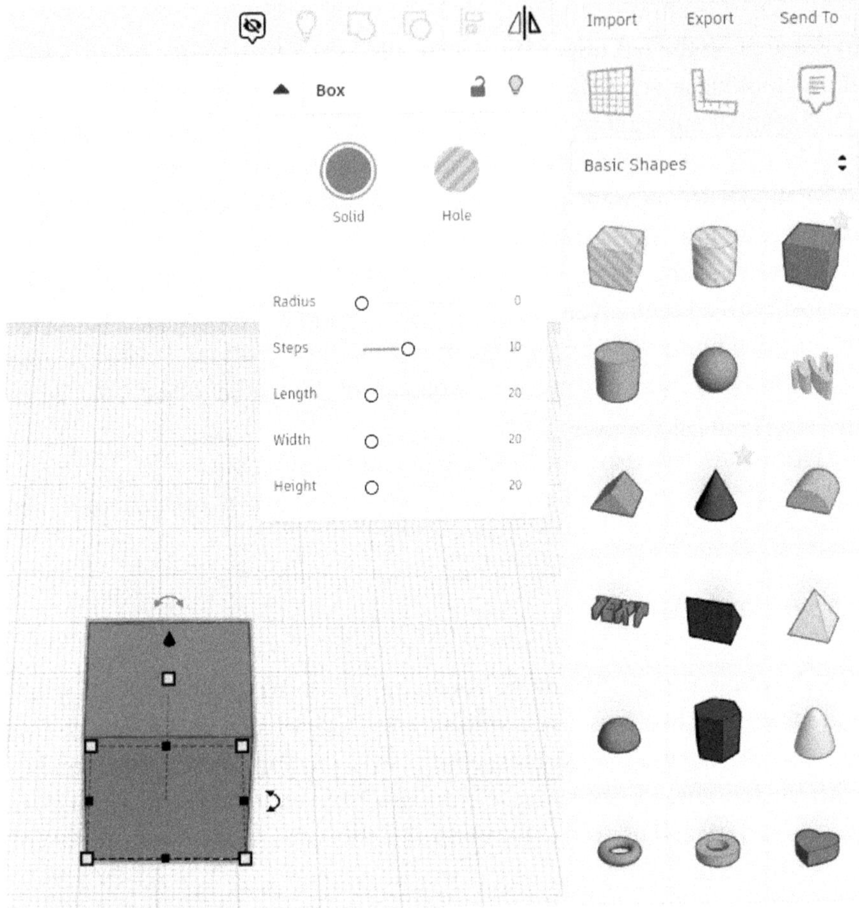

In the settings, you can define whether it should be a Solid or a Hole. Solid - adds material in the form of the object to another object, while Hole - subtracts the material from the other object. This will be clarified when you look at the Group/Alignment menu section.

If you want your red cube to have rounded edges, increase the radius scroll. And once you are happy with the changes, you can use the lock icon to prevent edits by mistake. Clicking the bulb icon makes the object disappear.

Besides the basic shapes like cubes, cylinders, spheres, etc., there are more complex objects you can try out by clicking the drop-down where it says Basic Shapes. You will find objects like creatures, everyday objects like cups, bottles, etc.

Workplane tools

On the right of the screen, just above the shapes, you will see three workplane tools: a new workplane, ruler, and notes tool.

With the new workplane tool, you can create a second workplane on the object. This is primarily used in scenarios when you want another offset plane to the original workplane to build a complex object.

When you click the ruler tool and move it to the workplane, you will see a coordinate system appear, allowing you to see the dimension of the object, like the length, width and height of the cube. And it also gives the distance between the object from the middle of the workplane. The dimensions are always in millimetres (mm).

Note tool is self-explanatory. You can use this to keep notes about the object or to-do tasks to do in the future.

Grid Option

Edit Grid option can be found at the bottom right. You can change the units here from millimetres to inches if you are inclined to do so, but I would strongly suggest not doing this as all slicers and most of the tools on the web use millimetres by default.

Also, if you are designing a large object, you can change the size of the workplane by changing the width and length to something higher than 200mm.

Just below the Edit Grid button, there is the Snap Grid option. Here you can set the steps in which the object should move in relation to the grid of the working plane. The lesser the value, the finer you can move the object. The default is set to a 0.1 mm interval, which is equal to the size of the smallest blue box on the workplane grid.

Group/Alignment Menu

On the top right, from left to right you will find options to Toggle notes visibility, show all, group, ungroup, align and mirror.

Group and Ungroup concepts are two most essential functions for building an object in Tinkercad. Let's take a look at an example - when you have to place a cylinder on top of a cube and make both these shapes into one object. Once you are done placing the cylinder on top of the cube, select both the shapes by clicking and drawing a rectangle to select both the objects, then click the group option. If the operation is successful, then both the shapes will form one object, with the same colour. In the picture below for a demonstration, the second object below is a duplicate of the first one, which was selected and grouped.

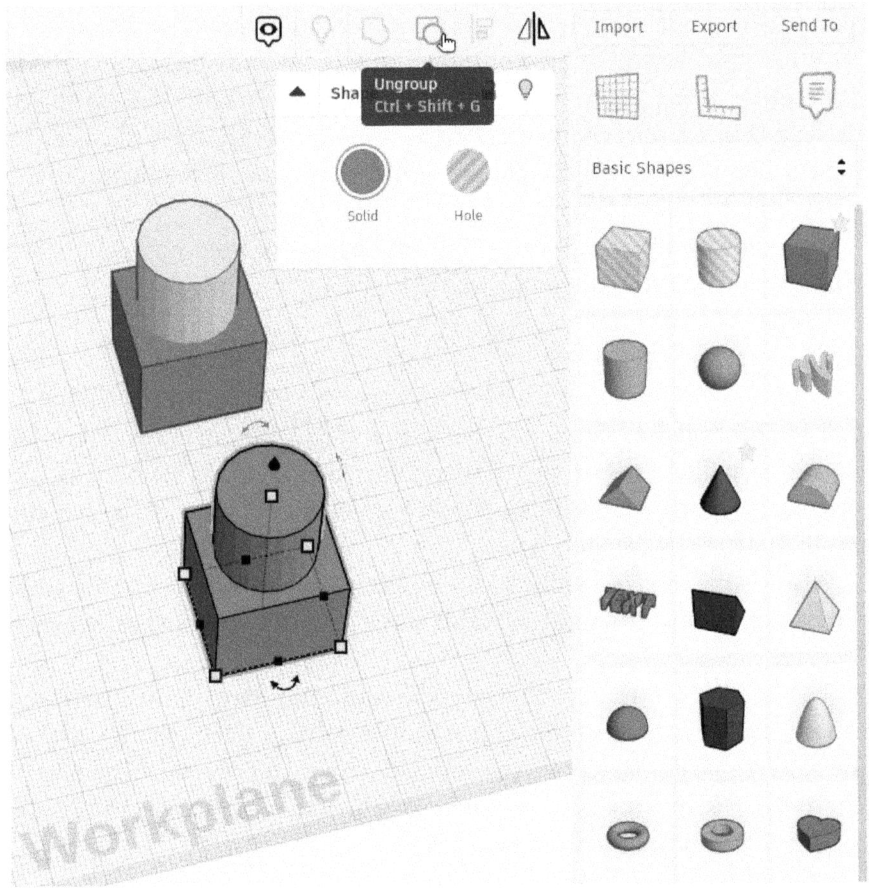

Say you have made a mistake and want to increase the height of the cylinder. You can select the object and then click ungroup, as shown in the picture. This will break the object back into a cube and cylinder.

In addition to group and ungroup, the Align function is widely used to align two or more objects. Similar to the example above, if you want to create a hole in the center of the cube, you would select a cube and a hole cylinder and add them to the workplane. Select both the cylinder and cube using the rectangular select, and click on the Align option. You should then see fields with black points. With the help of the black dots, you should be able to move the hole cylinder to the cube's center. You will first click the centre dot on the Y axis, followed by the center on the X axis, as shown in the picture.

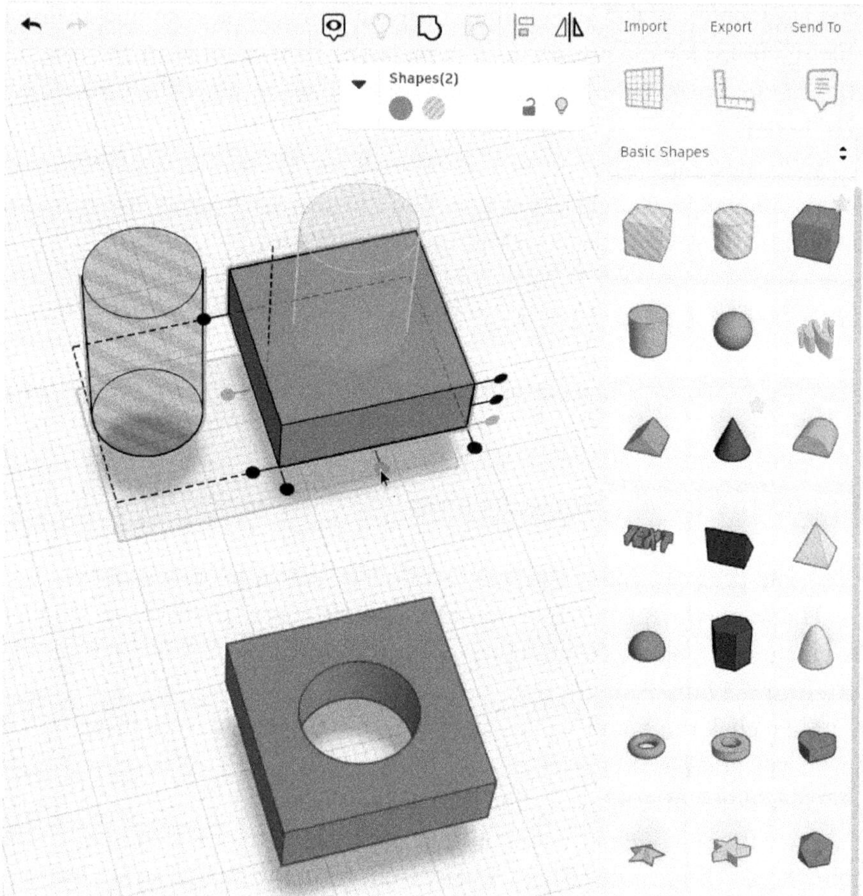

The last function is **Mirror**. This allows you to mirror an object and is similar to when you stand in front of a mirror with a T-shirt with wording on it the mirror shows the words in reverse.

Import/Export/Send To

On the right-hand side of the Group/Alignment Menu, you will see the Import, Export and Send To functions. With the export function, you can export existing objects on the workplane in STL format, which you then send to your slicer to get it ready for 3D printing.

With the import function, you can import an STL that you downloaded from the internet and modify to meet your needs. For example, consider you have downloaded a shelf bracket from Thingeverse.com and realised that the holes for the screws need to be larger. You can import the bracket STL file in Tinkercad and modify the screw holes to meet the screws you purchased.

With the Send To button, you can share your 3D creation with others via a link in email or Google Classroom. You can also, share your 3D object on sites like Thingeverse.com, MyMiniFactory.com, etc.

Hands-On 1 : Custom Key chain

Start by creating a new design.Change the name of your project to - Keychain.

Create the base of the Keychain

Click and drag a cylinder onto your workplane from the basic shapes.

Then drag the Ruler helper onto the workplane at the side of the cylinder to create a keychain base with precise measurement, set X,Y and Z values to 40 ,40 and 5 mm.

Then click the X and Y placement to the centre of the work plane, X is 0 and Y is 0 and Z is 0.

Once done, drag a hole cylinder to the workspace.

Since the ruler helper is still on, you will be able to set X = 34 mm, Y = 34 mm and Z = 5 mm, and also x,y,z placement from the middle as 3,3,3 mm.

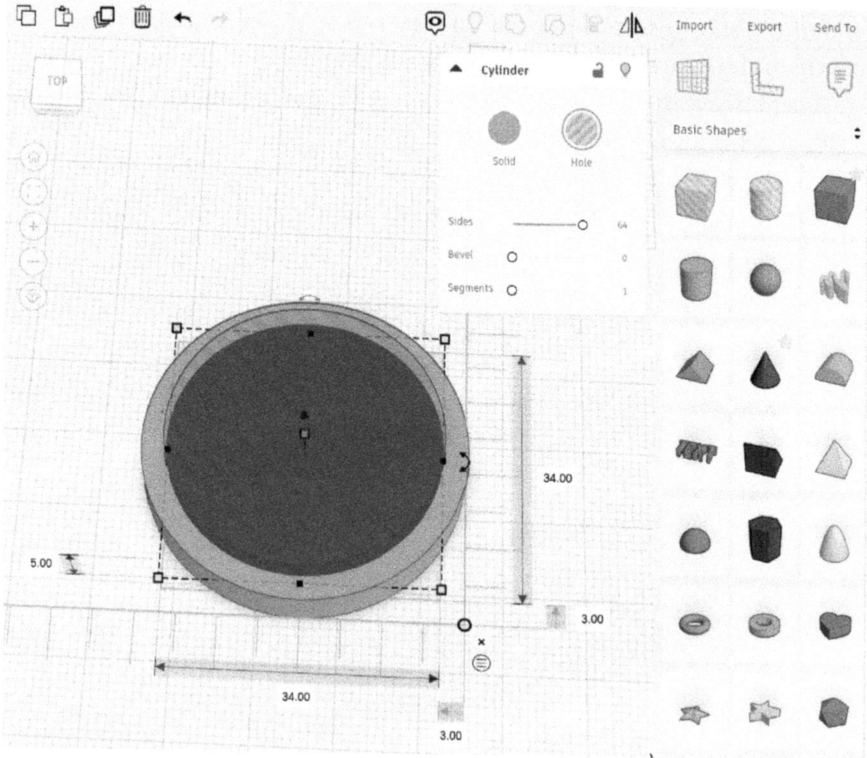

Once done, click the Group button in the top right. This will subtract the hole from the yellow base cylinder.

Creating a hole for the key ring

Drag another hole cylinder

With the ruler helper still on set X = 5 mm , Y = 5 mm , and Z = 10mm

And set the placement values as X = 32 mm, Y = 18 mm, and Z = -2 mm

Once done, click the Group button. This will create a hole for the key ring.

Add text to the tag

Drag a new workplane in the middle section of the name tag. Then click on the text shape, and drag it onto the new workplane.

In the text, properties change the text and type in your name. Click the end of the text to reduce the size and try and approximately move it to the centre of the base surface, as you see in the picture.

Ensure from the left-hand side Perspective menu, you have set it to the TOP, to make it easy to centre the text.

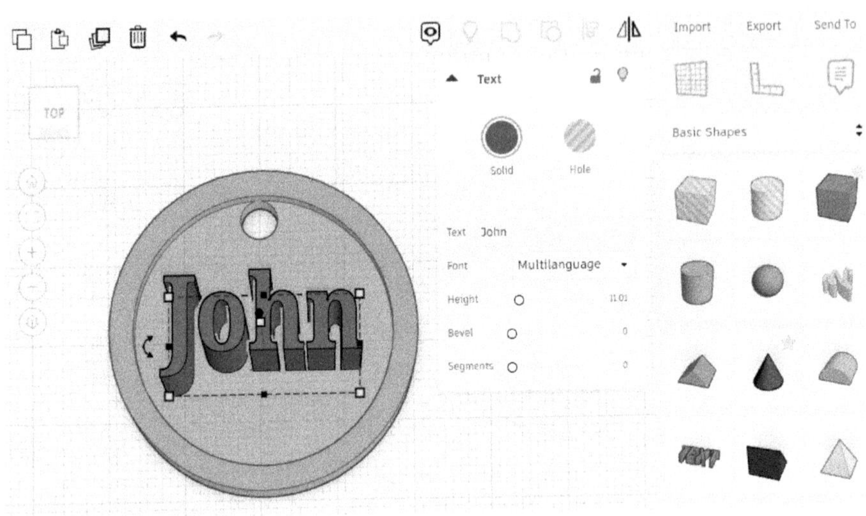

For minute movements, use the arrow keys on your keyboard.

Finally, select both the text shape and the base object and click group. This will change the colour of the text to the base colour.

Now click the export button and select the STL file option to export the STL.

Congratulations! you have created your first 3D design and are ready to slice the file and 3D print it.

Hands-On 2: Making a Phone Case

Before designing a case for your phone, find out the exact dimension. The phone cover designed below is for a phone with a length of 150 mm, a width of 75 mm and a height of 10 mm. And has a camera at the back with a USB C connector for charging at the bottom.

Start by creating a new design. Change the name of your project to - Phone Case.

Designing the base for the phone case

Drag a cube on the surface and modify the Length to 152 mm, Width to 77mm and Height to 12 mm. You can do this by typing in the number in the cube's parameters. If you observe the length, width and height, have 2 mm added to it, to account for the thickness of the phone case.

You now need to create an opening in the cube to put the phone in. The best way to do this is to use another hole cube and subtract it.

Let's add a hole cube with the length and width of the phone, and the height slightly higher to help with the subtraction. Set the Length to 150 mm, Width to 75 mm and Height to 14 mm

The next challenge is to bring both shapes, one on top of the other. The best way to do this is using the Align operation. Select both the shapes, click align, and click the centre dot on both the X and Y planes.

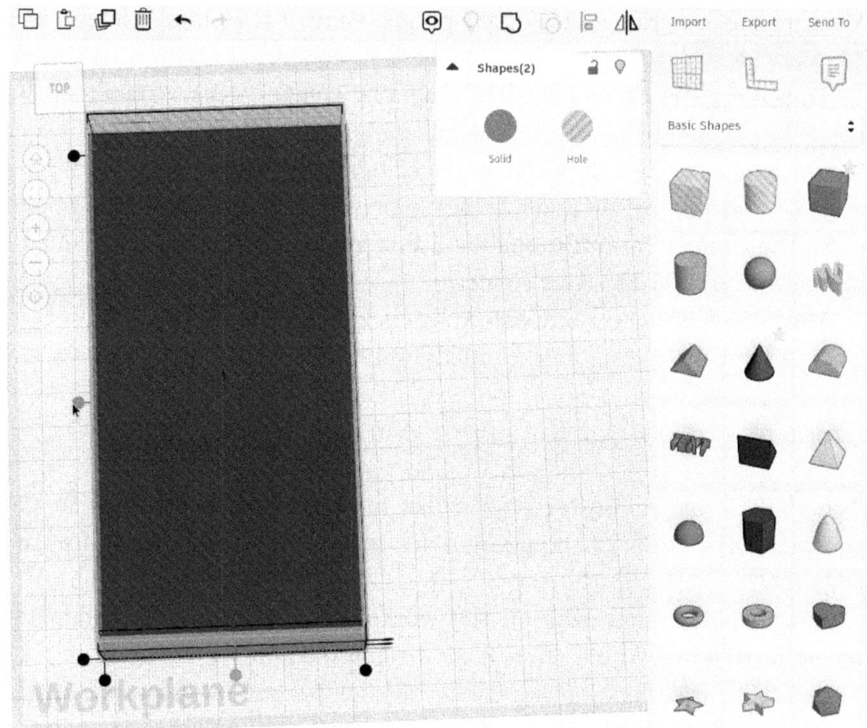

Once done, select the hole cube and click the black arrow to move it 2 mm higher from the work plane.

Now, if you hit the Group button, you should see the shell of your case created. But before you hit the group button, we need to account for the curves on the four corners of the phone.

Creating curved corners

Undo the group function by clicking on undo or pressing ctlr+z on your keyboard.

Click on the hole cube, and set the Radius parameter to 6

And then do the same for the cube below, set the Radius to 6

Now select both the objects and click Group.

Creating a cut-out for the camera lens

Measure the camera cut out for the phone. Here, it is 30 mm in length and 14 mm wide.

To achieve the camera cut-out, drag a hole cube to the surface, set the Length to 31 mm, Width to 15 mm and Height to 5 mm, and set a radius of 15mm, to accomodate the curve of the camera protrusion.

With the help of the Ruler helper, move the hole cube onto the phone case. The camera cut-out should be 5 mm away from the left edge and 14 mm down from the top right corner.

Move the hole cube 3 mm below, by clicking the top arrow.

And then click Group to execute the subtraction.

Creating cut-out for the phone charger

The USB C connection for power, like most phones, is precisely in the centre at the bottom of the phone. This makes it easy, as we can use the align tool.

Drag another hole cube on the workplane and change its parameter length to 10 mm, width to 25 mm and height to 6 mm.

Select the case and the hole cube, and click Align. Now select the phone case and press the center dot at the bottom of the case and the center dot at the height level of the case.

Then using your keyboard up/down arrow key moves the hole cube down till it cuts through the wall of the case, as you see in the picture below.

Once done, select both the objects and hit Group.

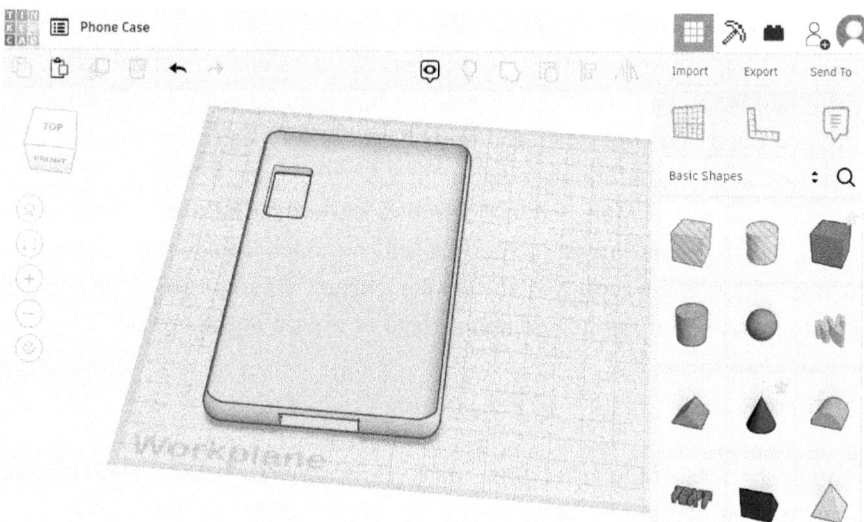

Your phone case is now ready. You can take this one step further and use the text shape and subtract it from the phone case below to add your name.

CHAPTER VIII

Common Mistakes and Solutions

To avoid unnecessary errors in 3D printing, it is vital to know the common mistakes you may encounter in 3D printing. As a beginner, here are a few mistakes with probable solutions.

Warping

If the 3D print cools too quickly and unevenly, parts of the print, mostly the edges, can detach from the print bed and curl upwards. This effect is called warping.

Root cause

Warping is caused by an inhomogeneous temperature in the printed object. Filament expands when heated and contracts when cooled. It would be ideal if the print had the same temperature from the first to the last layer.

In addition to the tilt of the print bed, that is one side of the bed is slightly lower than the other. If the distance between the nozzle and the print bed is too large, only a tiny part of the filament strand will adhere to the print bed and cool down too quickly on its way there. An optimal first layer is a key to avoiding warping.

Also, as your printer gets old, the bed starts heating unevenly in some cases. That is, one corner of the bed will be much cooler than the other, which will cause warping at the cooler corner. In some 3D printers, the cooling fan aims at the heated bed instead of the tip of the nozzle.

Solution

The best way to reduce warping once you have your print bed level is to increase the bed temperature in the slicer settings by increments of 5 °C. And also slow down the fan speed by increments of 10%.

Double-check your slicer setting that you have included some Build plate adhesion settings like Skirt or Brim.

Also, if the cooling fan is aiming at the bed instead of the nozzle, the best way to get around this is to 3D print a fan shroud instead of bending the metal or plastic that holds the fan. For the fan shroud, you can go to a 3D model repository site like thingiverse.com.

And during winters, if you live in cold climates, move your printer to an area with a room temperature of at least 25 °C.

Bed Adhesion – part being knocked over

Losing a print due to it not sticking to the print platform is a common issue and one that's usually relatively easy to resolve.

Also, it's not always the printer's fault, and if you've tried to print a model that only has a small amount of contact with the bed, then undoubtedly, your print will get knocked over.

Root cause

There could be multiple root causes for this issue, but it mainly occurs due to an unlevel print bed. If you had a 3D object printing perfectly a few weeks ago, the bed screws could get loose due to vibration.

Slicer settings are not proper, and the temperature of the nozzle is set to low. Or you are printing a 3D model with minimum contact with the bed. Imagine you're trying to print Scooby-Doo, the dog, and the only contact with the build surface is the dog's paws. Also, you have not checked the Generate Support in the slicer setting to add support under the head and belly of the dog.

Sometimes your build plate could be getting old or not clean. Or your Bed adhesion material like masking tape and glue stick needs to be reapplied.

Solution

The first thing to check if such an issue occurs is your bed levelling. Clean the build plate and apply new bed adhesion materials like masking tape and a glue stick. In addition, for the first layer to stick to the bed, try to reduce the speed of the initial layer in your slicer to 70% of the standard print speed.

In the case of a 3D model with the minimum amount of contact with the bed, change your slicer setting that we discussed in Chapter V, build plate adhesion needs to be set to brim. And also, check the Generate support setting to add support under the dog's head, tail, and belly.

Curling corners

The corners with sharp edges and overhangs curl up when the 3D object cooling is insufficient, and the extrusion temperature is too high. This gets worse as more layers are added, and the part can finally detach from the bed.

Root Cause

This mainly occurs because the cooling fan is slow. Or it also could be that the cooling fan is not aimed at the correct position. That is, it is aimed at the bed instead of the nozzle.

Another cause could be the temperature of your nozzle is set too high, leading to over extrusion of filament. And, if the cooling fan is too slow, curling up of the edges will be a common occurrence in 3D prints with sharp edges.

Solution

The quickest solution for this is to increase your fan speed. And also, improve the positioning of your cooling fan to the correct position by 3D printing a fan shroud. You should be able to find a 3D model to print for your fan on a site like thingiverse.com.

After calibrating your extruder and getting nozzle temperature under control, over extrusion should not be an issue.

Layer separation

Similar to bed adhesion, layer adhesion between two layers is about balancing the temperature and extrusion settings.

Root cause

If the print temperature of the nozzle is set too low, you have the potential of layers separating from each other and the 3D print breaking horizontally.

In addition, it could be that you are suffering from your print cooling too fast, causing your print to contract and causing layer separation mid-print. This is common for ABS prints.

Another cause of under separation is under extrusion mid-print. This could happen because of poor quality filament or dust and other debris in the nozzle.

Solution

The first thing to check if you come across layer separation is to increase your nozzle temperature by 5 °C increments. And when printing materials like ABS, to reduce the expansion and contraction rate, it is essential to have an enclosed 3D printer or build a 3D printed enclosure.

And also, ensure that your filament is of good quality.

Over/Under extrusion

A little bit of Over/Under extrusion can go unnoticed by the naked eye. But this becomes a severe issue if you have designed parts that go into each other, like a screw and a nut. If the parts are over extruded or under, the part will not fit together even though you had accounted for tolerance in design.

Root cause

Check if your nozzle is old and corroded to the point that the nozzle tip diameter has increased. Changes in nozzle diameter are not noticeable. An increase of 0.4 mm to 0.5 mm will not be noticeable.

This could also mean that your extruder gears are worn out or the tension spring on the extruder is too tight/loose.

Solution

Most 3D printers come with a brass nozzle, potentially needing replacement after eight months of regular printing.

Also, check that the extruder gears are not worn out or dust and debris are collected around its teeth.

If this issue is still not resolved, try to reduce/increase the flow % in slicer advance settings, it is default set to 100%.

Layer shifting

As the name suggests, Layer shifting can be a common occurrence if your printer speed is high. The part will either break horizontally or will turn out to be crooked.

Root Cause

This usually happens if your printer speed is too high. And, your steppers do not have sufficient torque to keep the pulley mechanism in the correct position. This causes the hotend to move away from its intended path.

In addition, as your printer gets old, your belt tension becomes loose to a point, causing the teeth of the belt to skip causing a layer shift.

Also, in rare cases when you're just getting started with your new printer, you will observe layer shifting because of a bad electrical connection at the stepper motor.

Solution

The first thing to do is reduce your speed by increments of 10 mm/s. And also, double-check your belt tension on all the axis, that is, x,y and z.

Nozzle Jam, extrusion stopped in the middle of the print

This can be the most frustrating issue, where filament stops oozing out from the hotend.

Root cause

There are multiple root causes for this issue. If the nozzle is too close to the bed, when the first layer is printing, the nozzle will clog because of too much back pressure.

If the extruder is left heated for extended periods, like 10-15 minutes, the plastic in the hotend will tend to burn to cause a jam. Bad quality filament is also another major cause of nozzle jams. And dust and debris can build up over time in the hotend, causing the nozzle to jam.

Solution

Based on the material you were using before the jam, increase the hotend temperature by at least 20 C using the menu on your 3D printer LCD screen, and now try to push the filament through the PTFE tube. For PLA, if you had your temperature set to 200 C in your slicer setting, now set it to 220 C.

If the jam isn't cleared, you will have to disassemble the hotend from the belt mechanism. Then, loosen the nozzle from the heater block. For this, heat the hotend and turn off the fans using your 3D printer LCD screen. Push the filament to see if the jam clears out.

If this does not work, you will have to remove the nozzle and clean it by passing a thin wire and then brushing it down.

Filament snaps

The filament spool looks full, and when you check, there appears to be filament in the feed tube, but nothing's coming out of the nozzle. This is more of an issue with Bowden type printers where the filament is hidden, so breakages aren't always immediately apparent.

Root cause

Several issues cause this, but primarily old or cheap filament. Although most filaments such as PLA and ABS do last a long time, if they're kept in the wrong conditions, such as, in direct sunlight or in a room where the humidity levels fluctuate, they can become brittle.

Another issue is filament diameter is not consistent at the end of the manufacturing company. This is rare today but can happen with the odd spool.

Solution

Remove the filament from the printer in the usual way, and clean your nozzle as there could be a possible nozzle jam. Remove the filament dust from the extruder gears. If the filament snapped inside the Bowden tube, you would have to remove the tube from the extruder and hotend. And remove the filament from the tube.

Now, try another filament spool, or better, to rule out any other issue with the print. Try an old spool from a week ago that you know was giving successful prints. Also, check smooth extrusion using the automatic extrude feature under the motion menu.

Ghosting or Ringing

Ghosting, also known as Ringing, echoing and rippling, is the presence of surface defects in prints due to vibrations in your 3D printer. You are likely to be seeing a repetition of lines or features across the exterior of a printed object, primarily when light is reflecting off your print at a certain angle.

Ghosting sometimes only affects certain parts of your prints. So some areas of your prints look perfect, while others look bad. It's especially prominent in prints that have wording engraved or a logo embossed into it.

Root cause

There can be multiple causes for this issue, including high print speeds. The build of your 3D printer, that is, the frame, is not well built and not rigid enough.

Due to the age of your printer, you could have a loose belt or loose a bed.

Solution

One of the solutions for this is to reduce your print speed in the slicer setting by increments of 10 mm/s. And also, check that your belts, bed, and other mechanical components mounted on the frame are tightened.

Stringing

Stringing occurs when small plastic strings are left behind on a 3D printed model. This is typically due to plastic oozing out of the nozzle while the extruder moves to a new location. This issue is also known as oozing, whiskers, or hairy 3D prints.

Root cause

The leading cause of this issue is that retraction settings are not up to the mark in your slicer. Retraction refers to filament being reversed by the extruder. In addition, if your temperature is too high, the hotend will continue to ooze filament when it travels from one part of the print to another.

Solution

To resolve the issue, double-check your retraction settings and try to reduce the hotend temperature in increments of 3 °C. This issue is a minor annoyance, and if the stringing effect is minimum, you don't have to worry. Just spend a few minutes after the 3D print, cleaning the part instead of changing the slicer settings.

Gaps in the Walls

Gaps are left in the walls of the 3D object inside. This is something you will have to keep an eye out for during the print, as the top and bottom layers of print tend to cover it up. Though this issue is not directly visible, it affects the strength of the 3D part.

Root cause

This issue mainly occurs because of wrong slicer settings concerning wall thickness. Let's consider a 3D part with a wall thickness of 1.8 mm, and say your layer lines are set to 0.4mm. The slicer will primarily create 4 shells in multiples of 0.4 mm, which leads to a wall thickness of 1.6mm with a 0.2 mm gap.

Solution

Get the slicer wall setting correct. In our above example, the ideal wall thickness would be 2 mm or in multiples Line Width of 0.4mm, in the slicer settings. Also, in its advanced setting, some slicers like Cura provide an option of Fill gaps between walls for safety set everywhere.

3D Model has Errors

This commonly happens in 3D scan models. Sometimes the scan is incomplete even though your machine/software shows 100% done, you have small holes, or a complete wall is missing.

Root cause

3D model errors occur because of small holes, missing walls and other minor mesh errors after your 3D scan is complete. Or if you download an STL from the internet that has never been 3D printed, this will either lead to slicer error, or the slicer software may crash.

Also, when designing a hollow part, if the wall thickness is set too low, say something like 0.2mm, which is less than the nozzle diameter of 0.4 mm, will undoubtedly cause the part to fail. This is pretty common in architecture design when you try to keep the walls of the inner rooms of the building to scale with the outer walls.

Solution

To fix issues with your scanned models, you can use the mesh tools software plugin with Cura slicer. This is something you will have to download and install. If this does not fix your issue, you will have to download software like Meshlab - www.meshlab.net, which provides tools for editing, cleaning, healing, inspecting, rendering, texturing and converting meshes. It offers features for processing raw data produced by 3D digitisation tools/devices and for preparing models for 3D printing.

In addition, for your designed hollow part like a snowman, ensure that your wall thickness is multiple of your nozzle diameter. A good starting point is at least 2mm.

Now, if you have observed, most issues with your 3D prints can be resolved by dialling in your slicer setting, which comes with experience and an abundance of patience. Remember, trying to fix one issue can cause the other. For example, if you are trying to fix Stringing problems which can be a minor annoyance, reducing the print temperature may lead to bed adhesion issues. This means finding the sweet spot with every slicer setting is essential.

CHAPTER IX

Maintaining your 3D Printer

Like any machinery with moving parts, a 3D printer demands regular maintenance from its users to avoid bad quality prints and frequent expensive repairs. Here are a few pointers that will help you maintain your 3D printer for the long run.

Before you carry out any maintenance on your 3D printer, unplug it from the power supply.

Keep your printer bed clean.

If the print bed is not cleaned, it will result in improper prints. If you have applied glue to the bed to avoid warping, the build plate can be cleaned by using a clean cloth and dipping the plate in warm water.

Clear any dust and debris from the Extruder mechanism

The extruder gear is the key to your 3D printer reliably pushing filament. Gears have sharp teeth to have a firmer grip on the filament, but they can't push through filament if there's a nozzle jam. And, the gears end up stripping the filament and get filled with filament dust. Clearing the jam at the nozzle won't be the end of it, as now the gears will need to be cleaned out before you can print again.

For cleaning the gear, you can use a toothbrush to ensure that the extruder functions smoothly and generates quality printouts.

Check that your bed is level regularly

3D printers move and vibrate, and the wingnuts/thumbscrews shake themselves loose over time. You will have to use the paper method once a week to check your bed level. You will mostly observe that you need a couple of turns of bed levelling knobs to get it levelled. Also, when moving the printer from one location to another, it is a good idea to check the bed level before starting a print.

Another way around this is to buy a bed levelling sensor that you can install at the side of your hotend.

Clean or replace your nozzle

By cleaning the filament nozzle of your printer, you will ensure that the printer's print quality is not hampered. The best way to judge a clogged nozzle is to see whether there is a curve while the filament comes down from the nozzle. If your 3D printer just isn't printing well after six months of use, a nozzle swap is what you may need.

In addition, if you are printing with corrosive materials like carbon fiber and using the standard brass nozzle that comes by default with your printer, you may have to replace your nozzle every week. To avoid this, buy a hardened nozzle.

Inspect if the cooling fans are still running

Over time, dust and filament debris can get on the fan blades and in the motor housing, causing the fan to jam. Depending on the make of your printer, you will have 3 or 4 small fans. You should feel the airflow on your hand for the circuit board fans. But in the case of the hotend fans, they should start spinning as soon as the temperature of the hotend goes above 70 °C.

See if there are any obstructions in the fan. If there are, remove them with a tweezer. If the fan is still not spinning, the fan needs to be replaced.

Tighten up your belts

Since the belts are constantly in motion, they tend to stretch over a period of time. A quick way to properly tension is to tighten any belt tensioners to the point that the carriages stick and don't move smoothly, then slowly loosen the tension just to the point where it runs well again.

In addition, a way to tell that your belts are at the end of their lifespan is if the belt completely snaps or visibly stretches or if your 3D prints are significantly over or under-sized. In this case, you will have to order new belts and replace them. You should still be able to use the old belt tensioners.

Lubricate Your 3D Printer

As a 3D printer is made up of numerous metal moving parts, it can lead to stoppages. To avoid such a situation, you must lubricate the 3D printer. For lubricating the printer, you can use sewing oil. A couple of drops on the rails and rods should do the trick.

Also, before you oil the rod and rails, check for dust and other filament debris and clean it with a dry cloth before oiling.

Replace the Bed surface

Over time, the bottom of your 3D prints tend to look rough. This is because your bed surface area has got scratched to the point that it needs replacement. You should be able to find replacement bed surfaces on e-commerce sites like Amazon, Flipkart, etc.

Update the 3D Printer Firmware

A 3D printer is not different from a home computer/laptop, which must be updated to function correctly. But before you update the firmware, it is always a good idea to go to the manufacturer's website and read the release note to read about the new features. And also, do a quick search for issues with the unique firmware release number. If there is nothing major, you can go ahead and update the firmware of your 3D printer.

Storing used filament

For a couple of weeks, if your freshly opened 3D filament is kept in a humid environment, you will observe that your filament gets hard and brittle and snaps when you try and twist it. Keep your filament in a vacuum-sealed/ zip-lock bag to prevent damage/deterioration.

CHAPTER X

Future of 3D Printing

We are living in a fascinating time! Based on the last decade of improved 3D printer technology, the future is bright. This technology is going to impact every human being on a global scale. In contrast, most academicians will tell you that 3D printing is another fad, and it will pass. You need to take a closer look at the development of personal computing, its meteoric rise today, where almost everyone has a personal computer in their pocket, called a Smartphone.

As seen in Chapter I, 3D printing is starting to find applications in many different industries, from Medicine to Manufacturing and Architecture. Based on the 3D design tutorial in the book, you would have realised how 3D printing can increasingly allow companies and individuals to create a new niche, customised and self-made products.

So continuing with the same thought to scale, the first industry that 3D printing will affect is Manufacturing. Once the technology stabilises, it will completely change the way things are made. Manufacturers being able to build most parts in-house will eliminate the long, complicated, and expensive supply chain and shipping process.

In addition, today, many industrial processes consume significant quantities of raw material as most of the current production uses subtractive manufacturing like cutting, filing, drilling and operating CNC machines to remove material from a block. As more and more 3D materials/filaments are invented, 3D printing will inherently be a more resource-efficient manufacturing process.

With 3D printing allowing for more customisation to a finished product, this will mean that consumers will get specialised products that fit their needs, which are potentially a lot cheaper. As our example in the medical field in Chapter I, every child who needs a prosthetic arm will be able to have one specifically customised to their liking, and the arm can be quickly redesigned and reprinted as they grow.

3D printing would possibly eliminate old jobs and replace them with new ones. It will also bring about a change and create new laws, especially related to intellectual property/patents. The exchange of 3D objects online additionally raises a broader question of how intellectual property may be controlled. Due to 3D scanning, protecting the intellectual property of physical things will prove very difficult in the long term.

As the technology improves, 3D printing will facilitate increased recycling and the ease of repair. Enabling localisation and manufacturing on-demand will allow a more sustainable and environment-friendly future.

Glossary

Archaeology

The scientific study of material remains (such as tools, pottery, jewellery, stone walls, and monuments) of past human life and activities.

AutoCAD

AutoCAD is a commercial computer-aided design and drafting software application. Developed and marketed by Autodesk. AutoCAD was first released in December 1982 as a desktop application running on microcomputers with internal graphics controllers.

Biodegradable

An object capable of being decomposed by bacteria or other living organisms and thereby avoiding pollution.

Bowden tube

Bowden tube encases the filament to transport it from the extruder motor to the hot end. Normally made of Teflon material.

CNC machines

CNC stands for Computer Numerical Control. CNC machines are electro-mechanical devices that manipulate machine shop tools using computer programming inputs. CNC machines are used to mill and process various materials, including wood, metals, and plastics.

Firmware

In computing, firmware is a specific class of computer software that provides low-level control for a device's specific hardware. Mostly etched directly into a piece of hardware

Intellectual property

Refers to creations of the mind, such as inventions, literary and artistic works, designs, symbols, names and images used in commerce.

G-Code

G-code can be described as commands for a machine (3D printer,CNC machine)that instructs it to perform actions like moving components, extruding filament, and so on. While most makers don't directly interact with G-code, every time you set a temperature, position, or start a print, you're sending G-code commands to your printer.

Kickstater

Is a global crowdfunding platform focused on creativity.

Laser Cutting

Laser cutting is a technology that uses a laser. Laser beam is directed at the material, which then either melts, burns, vaporizes away, or is blown away by a jet of gas, leaving an edge with a high-quality surface finish.

Maker

The Maker movement is a cultural trend that places value on an individual's ability to be a creator of things as well as a consumer of things. In this culture, individuals who create things are called Makers

Moulding

Moulding is the process of manufacturing by shaping liquid or pliable raw material using a rigid frame called a mould.

Open-Source

Open-source hardware/software is computer-related hardware/software that is released under a license, in which the copyright holder grants users the rights to use, study, change, and distribute the software and its source code to anyone and for any purpose.

Orthographic view

An Orthographic view (or projection) of a 3D scene is a 2D picture of it in which parallel lines appear parallel, and all edges perpendicular to the view direction appear in proportion, at exactly the same scale.

Patents

A Patent is an exclusive right granted for an invention, which is a product or a process that provides, in general, a new way of doing something.

Photopolymer

A Photopolymer is any type of material that experiences a direct or indirect interaction with light to change its physical or chemical properties.

Perspective

Perspective view is a two-dimensional representation of a three-dimensional space, where the apparent size of an object decreases as its distance from the viewer increases.

Prototype

A Prototype is an early sample, model, or release of a product built to test a concept.

Rapid prototyping

Rapid prototyping is the fast fabrication of a physical part, model or assembly using 3D Computer-Aided Design (CAD).

RepRap

RepRap is an abbreviation for "replicating rapid prototype". This phrase originated from the RepRap project, an initiative to make low-cost, open-source, mostly self-replicating 3D printers.

Retraction

In 3D printing, retraction is the extruder reversing the direction of the filament (i.e. pulling it away from the hot end). Typically, this is done in short bursts between consecutive instances of extrusion.

STEM

These are the kinds of skills that students develop in Science, Technology, Engineering, and Maths, including computer science.

STL

STL is a file format commonly used for 3D printing and Computer-Aided Design (CAD). The name STL is an acronym that stands for stereolithography — a popular 3D printing technology.

Thermoplastic

Is a plastic polymer material that becomes pliable or mouldable at a certain elevated temperature and solidifies upon cooling

Thing

A 3D printed object is referred to as a Thing in 3D printing terminology.

References

History of 3D printing

- https://en.wikipedia.org/wiki/3D_printing
- https://en.wikipedia.org/wiki/Computer-aided_design
- https://reprap.org/wiki/RepRap

Download 3D Design - STL files

- https://www.thingiverse.com/
- https://www.yeggi.com/
- https://www.myminifactory.com/
- https://www.shapeways.com/about
- https://pinshape.com/3d-marketplace

CAD tools

- https://www.tinkercad.com/
- https://en.wikibooks.org/wiki/OpenSCAD_Tutorial/Chapter_1
- https://www.sketchup.com/
- https://www.autodesk.com/products/fusion-360/overview
- https://www.solidworks.com/product/solidworks-3d-cad
- https://www.rhino3d.com/learn/

Slicing software

- https://ultimaker.com/software/ultimaker-cura
- https://slic3r.org/about/

- https://www.simplify3d.com/

3D printing Materials

- https://en.wikipedia.org/wiki/3D_printing_filament
- https://en.wikipedia.org/wiki/Polylactic_acid
- https://en.wikipedia.org/wiki/Acrylonitrile_butadiene_styrene

Slicing STL files

- https://support.ultimaker.com/hc/en-us/sections/360003548339-Ultimaker-Cura
- https://github.com/slic3r/Slic3r/wiki/Documentation
- https://en.wikipedia.org/wiki/G-code
- 3D Benchy - https://www.thingiverse.com/thing:763622
- Cura Mesh tool plugin - https://github.com/fieldOfView/Cura-MeshTools
- MeshLab - https://www.meshlab.net/

3D design - Tinkercad

- https://www.tinkercad.com/learn/designs/learning
- https://www.tinkercad.com/learn/designs/projects
- https://blog.tinkercad.com/tag/tips-tricks

www.ingramcontent.com/pod-product-compliance
Ingram Content Group UK Ltd.
Pitfield, Milton Keynes, MK11 3LW, UK
UKHW021924190726
13853UKWH00002B/833

9 798887 176734